THE BURDEN

Leadership with a Cross at the Center

TO: michael.

Sept 10/10

May all your burdens,
Be as wings are to a bird,
Or as sails are to a ship,
To carry you forward,
To your rest in Christ.

Charles E. Jackson

Charles E. Jackson

THE BURDEN
Leadership with a Cross at the Center

ISBN-13: 978-1-77069-083-7

Printed in Canada.

Word Alive Press
131 Cordite Road, Winnipeg, MB R3W 1S1
www.wordalivepress.ca

Mixed Sources
Cert no. SW-COC-001271
© 1996 FSC

BACK COVER PICTURE:
CHRIST CARRYING THE CROSS

The original bronze sculpture of the cover photograph was made from melted cannon shells by Emil St. Mirtschev of Sofia, Bulgaria in 1991. The photograph was taken by Christian Popkes, a young photographer in Hamburg.

The artists of Bulgaria, who had no work permits during the period of Communism, have very often expressed their time of suffering in the Christian motifs of the suffering Christ. Prints of the photograph are sold to benefit the work of the Baptist Union of Bulgaria. Used with permission.

Dedicated to all who take up the burden
of Christ in faith with thanksgiving.

"Whoso looketh to the white side of Christ's cross, and can
take it up handsomely with faith and courage, shall find it
such a burden as sails are to a ship, or wings to a bird."

—*SAMUEL RUTHERFORD, Letter LXXI*

"If any want to become my followers, let them deny themselves and take up their cross and follow me."

—MARK 8:34

CONTENTS

INTRODUCTION

A burden is something that is carried which has weight or substance. Jesus carried a cross. It was a burden to him. Every follower of Christ carries a cross. It is a burden to them. We come to Christ with our burden of sin and we find rest as he promised (Matthew 11:28-30). Those who are called to follow Christ and to lead others in the church take up another burden. The burden is the cross of Christ. Jesus called it light because he carries most of the weight, but it is nevertheless a burden.

The following articles and sermons were originally written, and in some cases preached, to alert the people of God to the possibility that to be a follower of Christ is costly.

These reflections come as a result of a prayerful concern for the church. They have also come from the burden of pastoral ministry, a heart that has felt the burden, but has also known the blessing of the Lord. Any pain or sorrow endured have in the end been translated and transformed into praise and thanksgiving as one realizes the privilege of carrying the cross after Christ.

I commend the following to the reader for whatever ministry God may be willing and able to impart through his blessed Holy Spirit. Thanks be to God.

REV. DR. CHARLES E. JACKSON, Pastor

Easter, 2010

ONE

A Biblical Lament

My brothers and sisters, I have great sorrow and unceasing anguish in my heart for God's people according to the Spirit. They are God's children, chosen and adopted, heirs of God and joint heirs with Christ. The crown has fallen from our head; woe to us, for we have sinned! Because of this our hearts are sick, because of these things our eyes have grown dim. We see not our signs; there is no longer any prophet, and there is no one among us who knows how long. How long, O God, is the foe to scoff? Is the enemy to revile your name forever? Will you not revive us again, so that your people may rejoice in you? In our own time revive your work; in our own time make it known; in wrath may you remember mercy.

They made me keeper of the vineyards, but my own vineyard I have not kept! I am no prophet, nor a prophet's son, and the Lord said to me, "Go, prophesy to my people." I will stand at my watchpost, I will keep watch to see what he will say to me. He has told you, O mortal, what is good; and what does the Lord require of you but to do justice, and to love kindness and to walk humbly with your God? Your people who talk together say to one another, each to his neighbour, "Come and hear what the word is that comes from the Lord." They come to you as people come, and they sit before you as my people, and they hear your words, but they will not obey them. When this comes—and come it will!—they shall know that a prophet has been among them.

The harvest is past, the summer is ended, and we are not saved. The righteous perish and no one takes it to heart. Is there no balm in Gilead? Is there no physician there?

Why then has the health of my poor people not been restored? But this I call to mind, and therefore I have hope: The steadfast love of the Lord never ceases, his mercies never come to an end; they are new every morning; great is your faithfulness.

I know the plans I have for you, says the Lord, plans for your welfare and not for harm, to give you a future with hope. Restore us to yourself, O Lord, that we may be restored; renew our days as of old. Not to us, O Lord, not to us, but to your name give glory, for the sake of your steadfast love and your faithfulness. A highway shall be there, and it shall be called the Holy Way; the unclean shall not travel on it, but it shall be for God's people. Therefore the Lord waits to be gracious to you; therefore he will rise up to show mercy to you. You shall weep no more. He will surely be gracious to you at the sound of your cry; when he hears it, he will answer you. For you have delivered my soul from death, and my feet from falling, so that I may walk before God in the light of life.

Jerusalem [Church], Jerusalem [Church]… How often have I desired to gather your children together as a hen gathers her brood under her wings, and you were not willing! See, your house is left to you, desolate… until you say, 'Blessed is the one who comes in the name of the Lord. [1]

TWO

The Burden
of Ministry

The burdened servant can be a pastor, a minister, a priest, or a full or part-time worker in the service of the Lord Jesus Christ in any place or capacity. He or she will encounter problems and stresses not found in any other vocation, career, or calling. There seems to be something peculiar to Christian ministry that brings out the best and worst in human nature. But once the mantel of ministry is taken up, something mysterious comes with it.

BURDENED

The true servant of the Lord will feel burdened or weighted down by the cares and concerns of their ministry, whatever it might be. The burden will be given by the Holy Spirit, slowly or quickly, with a realization that something has been placed on the soul that did not exist before. The burden is not like the weight of a backpack weighing one down or holding one back. It is taken on willingly, as a volunteer in the service of the King. *"And one does not presume to take this honor, but takes it only when called by God, just as Aaron was"* (Hebrews 5:4).

But the burden is not transferable or excusable. It is not like taking off a uniform at the end of the day. It is not like ending a shift when someone else takes over the job. There are no vacations or days off from this burden.

However one tries to get out of it, there is no turning back. Paul said that along with the external problems and suffering he faced, *"I am under daily pressure because of my anxiety for all the churches"* (2 Corinthians 11:28).

This can best be described as an ache of the soul, a burning of the spirit, an underlying concern that one carries. Mostly, it is invisible. There are no external markings, and no ways of knowing just what is exercising the servant of the Lord. Others might detect an overarching seriousness, a withdrawal from casual social contact or flippant conversation. There will probably be a desire to talk about spiritual matters or concerns about ministry, coupled with a desire to withdraw from public exposure to pour out the burden to the Lord Jesus in prayer.

BOTHERED

Essentially, the saint or servant of the Lord has been given a burden from the Lord, which bothers him or her to the point of consuming their life. Certain things bother them. Among these will be the sin of God's people, the decadence of the church, the evil trends of a godless and wicked society, the lack of holiness and health in God's servants, and the social, economic, political, and spiritual ills of the culture around them.

All of these things will bother the servant of the Lord to the point of involvement, correction, condemnation, and judgment of them in the name of the Lord.

But the bother will contain a genuine compassion and love for the souls of others with a longing to do something about it. As Ezekiel said of the exile of his people, *"I came to the exiles... And I sat there among them, stunned, for seven days"* (Ezekiel 3:15). As Jeremiah complained to God, *"I did not sit in the company of merrymakers, nor did I rejoice; under the weight of your hand I sat alone, for you had filled me with indignation"* (Jeremiah 15:17).

BORED

There is a boring part to the ministry, even one burdened by the Holy Spirit's concern.

The boring aspect of ministry comes from the routine, the repeated, and the regular duties of a servant of God. The Old Testament priest got bored with the same old, same old of the sacrificial system. There can be an "altar burn," or a getting too close to holy things, which can bring a familiarity and "take for granted" attitude that may be dangerous and even merit condemnation or a warning from God. This is the result of the boredom of doing the same things over and over again.

Some biblical examples suffice to give us a view of this condition. Moses' brother and sister got bored with his leadership and challenged his authority and God's choice. King Saul tried to shortcut Samuel's instructions from the Lord and offer his own sacrifices, with disastrous results. In the New Testament, Ananias and Sapphira (Acts 5) tried to keep back part of their intended offering to God and got caught by the Holy Spirit.

Simon Magus (Acts 8) thought the Holy Spirit's power could be bought with money. Demas got bored with Paul's routine and fell back in love with the world and deserted him (2 Timothy 4:9-10).

BROKEN

The burdened heart will also become the broken heart, crushed and bothered by the concerns of the church and the calling of ministry. Jesus said, *"Unless a grain of wheat falls into the earth and dies, it remains just a single grain; but if it dies, it bears much fruit"* (John 12:24). Both Henri Nouwen's book on helping those who have been broken and the J.B. Phillips biography of his personal struggle of trying to live a 130% life are titled *The Wounded Healer*. It often happens that the heart that has been wounded and broken spiritually is the one that can most be used in the service of Christ. Paul said, *"I have been crucified with Christ"* (Galatians 2:19), and it is by the cross of our Lord Jesus Christ that *"the world has been crucified to me, and I to the world"* (Galatians 6:14). Brokenness seems to be on the pathway to usefulness and blessedness. Count on it.

Blessed

The servant of the Lord will be blessed by taking on the burden of the Lord. There will be a freedom, an authority, a power, a closeness of fellowship which none but his loved ones know in ministry. The servant becomes the apple of God's eye that he delights to use for his glory and reward with his grace and presence.

There is a holy fragrance and odour on one who is blessed and gets closer to the fire of God than most by holy obedience. It is not sought after or earned, but is given as a sacred reward by the Master. There is no arrogance or holier-than-thou attitude expressed, but a shrinking from the limelight and a shyness and even a blush about any praise.

When Moses came down from the mountain, he did not know that his face shone! At this stage, a holy fear comes over the recipient, not wanting to displease the Lord or lose the blessing. I recall when A.W. Tozer's church in Toronto experienced revival shortly before his death in 1963. The prayer meeting increased from fifty to over two hundred people during the mid-week. People were saved, blessed, healed, and called at those meetings. Not wanting to miss out nor hinder the blessing, he took himself out of the leadership so that he could soak up the blessings of what God the Holy Spirit was doing there. Those who were involved would not dare miss a meeting for fear of losing out on something special God was going to do. Many of us young people were called, filled, and began training for Christian ministry because of those fragrant days when God was precious and his anointing was near.

THREE

A Head Banger
for Jesus

I gave up. I quit. I got out of the church and left the pastorate. I was fed up and had enough of banging my head against the wall of the structure that would not change.

Just to be honest and to clarify, I didn't really resign. I retired, but it was for the same reason. The politics, the resistance, the putting off, the excuses all added up to the same, year after year for most of my ministry. Congregations like things the way they are. In a sense, it was, "as it was in the beginning, is now, and forever will be, world without end."[2] I was tired of being a head banger for Jesus and wanted out.

It wasn't always like this. When I started out over thirty years ago, I was idealistic, visionary, energized and worked at, and prayed for revival, renewal, and a revitalization of the local church. I was trained, full of ideas, and ready to take on the world, the flesh, and the devil with Spirit-filled preaching and devoted leadership. I wanted to see souls saved and come to the Saviour. I wanted to see the church grow and to give glory to God the Father.

Through positions in youth work, Christian Education, and a pastor in single and multi-staffed churches, I worked hard under God and in the power of the Holy Spirit to see something happen for good and the kingdom.

So now that I have come to the twilight of my ministry for Christ, and I wonder what is next, I must ask myself if all those years were fruitless, without souls, and the goodness and blessing from the Lord. Certainly there were highlights, blessing and fruit in abundance, though often unseen and unknown at the time. Time and experience have brought most of the misgivings around to show that the hand of the Lord had really been upon me all along and that Jesus was still building his church and not even hell could stop it, let alone my scepticism and frustrations.

But how long did I have to be a head banger for Jesus? The surprising answer is—for the duration, to the end, until Jesus comes again or calls me home. Let me explain. The apostle Paul, in a very positive and optimistic section of Romans, talks about how nothing can separate us from the love of Christ and says, *"For your sake we are being killed all day long; we are accounted as sheep to be slaughtered"* (Romans 8:36).

He is quoting a double reference from Psalm 44:11 and 22. The allusion is to being expendable, exposed, and even exiled from God and his cause, both as a people and as a nation. Paul uses this to convince the Roman Christians and us that *"in all these things we are more than conquerors through him who loved us"* (Romans 8:37).

The message to me, and to any in leadership in the church today, is the same as it has always been—You are a head banger for Jesus; take it, accept it, and suffer it for the sake of Christ and his body. You were called to this.

Even if the church is declining and dying, if its people are sinful and disobedient, if they refuse to budge, budget, or bend to your great plans and wonderful new Christ-centred vision for the future, this is your burden to bear, even if the church is to blame.

This is the cross you are to carry. You are expendable. You may become fodder in the fight or a casualty of the war. You may become wounded and have to withdraw from the action. Or else you could desert and quit in the heat of battle, or even retire.

So suck it up and stop complaining. Remember, you are a head banger for Jesus! Learn to love it. As far as I can tell, there were only two leaders in the New Testament who were told ahead of time what they would have to suffer for the Kingdom's sake—Paul and Jesus. It is assumed that when the call came to the rest and to us, whatever the cost, it was part of the deal—no reserve, no retreat, and no regrets.

What will it be then? Sure, you should seek and pray for all the changes that will make the modern church a more viable instrument in the hands of the Holy Spirit for the salvation of the nations—seeker sensitive, purpose driven, emergent, contemporary, or blended worship, youth oriented or whatever. But keep in mind, you may be one of the chosen ones who will never have their name up in lights, as few of us will. Instead, you may labour in your own part of the vineyard, seen only by the Vine grower, producing fruit that will be all the more precious on *"the day of the Lord's coming"* (2 Timothy 1:12, 4:8).

NOTE: The writer returned to the pastorate after one year of retirement.

FOUR

Christ Abuse[3]

We hear about the abuse of children and the elderly and it irritates us. We read about the sexual and emotional abuse of spouses and we are angered. There is protest against political, social, economic, and environmental abuse and we applaud it.

But who knows about or cares about Christ abuse? And yet, probably at no time in the history of the western church has Christ been abused as he is today! How so?

Christ abuse comes in the form of the New Atheism, which questions not only the existence of God, but also the incarnation and deity of Jesus the Son of God. In reality, it is the old liberalism and humanism dressed up in modern couture seeking admittance into the mainstream of credible intellectual academia. But it nevertheless undermines and questions the simple faith of those who have not or are not able to visit the hallowed halls of learning with the latest critical methodology. With Doctors and Reverends and Bishops before their names, they are able to capture the attention of a religious world hungry for the latest shot or injection into the mysteries of God, into which they have been trained and have made promises to keep and to uphold. We call this trend Christ abuse.

Christ abuse can come from within the fold, as with the Jesus Seminar group of theologians who try to separate what Jesus actually said from what the church said he said in the New Testament documents. They even vote on selected texts with a colour bead scheme.

Christ abuse can come from commentators, interpreters, and translators of the Word when they devalue it in the eyes and understanding of the people. It was thought, and we were told, that the newer and up-to-date translations of the Bible would invariably make it easier for the general public and Christians both to read and to understand God's Word. Instead, there is no longer any standard reference point that all Christians can refer to or memorize with any amount of certainty or authority. And the modern Power Point presentations mean that Bibles no longer need to be supplied or carried to churches because any text or translation can be projected on the overhead screen(s) so as to be seen by everyone.

Clergy become Christ abusers when they take advantage of their sacred office and calling and cross the boundary lines by abusing parishioners either physically, mentally, or spiritually to their own ends. This is a scandal on the church of whatever stripe or denomination and brings scathing ridicule and scorn on the whole bride of Christ by the incredulous world.

Congregations become Christ abusers when they beat up on their pastors in an effort to settle a conflict they perceive to be centred around him or her. New words such as "clergy killers" and "congregational killers" have sadly come into the vocabulary of the church to describe these phenomena.[4] Many pastors are beginning to take stress leaves and call 1-800 Employee Assistance Program numbers for emergency help in their crisis of abuse.

Christ abuse also appears in the local congregation where instead of loving one another people bite and devour one another (Galatians 5:14-15). Congregational infighting is devastating to church growth and spiritual expectations. This is how one commentator describes it:

> There can be no preaching in the wrong atmosphere. Our churches would be different places if congregations would only remember that they preach far more than half the sermon. In an atmosphere of expectancy the poorest effort can catch fire. In an atmosphere of critical coldness or bland indifference, the most spirit-packed utterance can fall lifeless to the earth.[5]

The apostle Paul talked about *"completing [in his flesh] what is lacking in Christ's afflictions for the sake of his body, that is, the church"* (Colossians 1:24). This is ongoing in the world today as faithful servants of God suffer affliction for the sake of Christ and his church. This is accepted and expected. But Christ abuse is different. Its manifest evil characteristic is that it is always against the will of God.

It is not God's will that his Word be abused or that the teachings and traditions of the church, for which Christ gave his life, be undermined and discredited.

It is not the Father's will that the body of Christ, represented by the local congregation, be abused. It is not the will of the Spirit of Grace that the servants of Christ be abused or become abusers of the body, or that church members abuse each other.

Christ abuse in inflicted knowingly, willingly, and maliciously against Christ, his church, his servants, his word, and against his people for whom his died. This is why it must be exposed, condemned, and resisted by those who know and love the truth.

Stop Christ abuse!

FIVE

The Church: From Grey to Green

Have you noticed how many grey heads are in the church today, of all denominations? In fact, on any given Sunday morning they are in the majority. What's going on? Isn't the church for all ages of people in all stages of life? And look at the pulpit. Most clergy, ministers, pastors, and leaders are changing from grey to white—the hair, I mean!

Something has happened in the last twenty years or so in the calling, training, and equipping of leaders for the church of the twenty-first century. I remember when most of my evangelical mentors and leaders were in the prime of their ministries: A.W. Tozer, Francis Schaeffer, Billy Graham, John Stott, Tony Compolo. Now, they are either gone to glory, or are in the twilight of their ministry and influence. So who is taking their place?

Much has been written about the greying of the church and the question asked about the next generation of leaders both in the pulpit and in the church. The question is, what do we do about it? How do we go from grey to green in the church? The answer is, God already has the situation in hand. When Jesus saw the crowds in his own time and ministry,

> he had compassion on them, because they were harassed and helpless, like sheep without a shepherd.
> Then he said to his disciples, "The harvest is plentiful but the laborers are few; therefore ask the Lord of the harvest to send out laborers into his harvest." (Matthew 9:36-38)

There are some simple observations that can be made from this statement:

Jesus loves us and sees our helpless and harassed condition. His heart of love goes out to his church, which he said he would build against all opposition, even hell itself. The harvest is the Lord's, not ours, which might be a surprise for some of us! Because Jesus is the same yesterday, today and forever, he knows our deepest and desperate need right now. There have always been fewer workers than needed. Jesus' disciples in every generation have a responsibility to ask for more help. He calls his own to enter into burden bearing and cross-carrying prayer. God is already at work to answer and supply.

How does this work biblically?

Before a man or woman of God departs the scene, God has someone already in the shadows to take over, even if the leadership has not been a good one. Consider the following examples: Joshua was in training to take over for Moses. Judges were raised up in response to the call of his hurting people as a bridge between Moses and the kings. Samuel was chosen and trained to take over from Eli and his wicked sons. David replaced Saul as king of Israel. Elisha was being primed to succeed Elijah when a chariot of fire took him away. John the Baptist was the important forerunner for Jesus and his ministry. Paul had Timothy and Titus as apostolic assistants to continue his itinerate work.

And church history is full of one leader following another in important areas of the work of the Lord. So what is happening today, and why have we come up short? We could look at the church itself and say it has been negligent in the recruiting, training, and the placing of candidates for ministry through its Bible College and Seminary system. We could look at Christians and say they lack the commitment and steadfastness of a former generation, which produced great leaders and saints. We could say this is a time of small things and that the church is in a free fall of decadence and self-centred arrogance. We could interpret our times in light of the church at Laodicea (Revelation 3:14-22) and say that our church is worldly, sinful, and indulgent. We could also say that our present generation has sold out to the cultural and societal dictates of our own day and age.

But what does the Lord say? He says the harvest time is now. It is always a time for harvest. He says it is his harvest. He knows shepherds are needed. We are to pray that he will act and send the leadership we need. We are to work in our own area of his harvest field and be faithful.

For the record, he could also say, "I already have a David learning to lead a small flock of sheep in obscurity. I have apprenticed a young man to a strong leadership mentor like Moses. I have an Elisha washing the hands of an Elijah. I have a Paul sharpening his intellectual skills in the best theological schools in the country. I have a forerunner preparing the way of the Lord for the next generation."

So what is the answer to the greying of the church in our times? The answer is that the church may look grey now, but there is a green shoot growing out of the dry ground.

The Spirit of the Lord is moving in hearts that love the Lord Jesus. He is the Spirit of wisdom and of understanding, the Spirit of counsel and power, the Spirit of knowledge and of the fear of the Lord (Isaiah 11:1-3).

The bones may look exceedingly dry, but there is a fresh breath coming to breathe new life into them (Ezekiel 37:1-14). There is a river flowing from the temple of God. The water goes from being ankle deep to knee deep, to waist deep, to a river that was deep enough to swim in (Ezekiel 47:1-12). *"The eyes of the Lord range throughout the entire earth, to strengthen those whose heart is true to him"* (2 Chronicles 16:9). *"Not by might, nor by power, but by my spirit, says the Lord of hosts"* (Zechariah 4:6). *"Yet I will leave seven thousand in Israel, all the knees that have not bowed down to Baal, and every mouth that has not kissed him"* (1 Kings 19:18). His word is: not everyone has sold out!

> If my people who are called by my name humble themselves, pray, seek my face, and turn from their wicked ways, then I will hear from heaven, and will forgive their sin and heal their land. (2 Chronicles 7:14)

This is the answer. Do we believe it? Will we live it and pray that we might see it happen in our time?

SIX

The Portrait
of a Prophet

It is time for a prophet to rise again from the midst of God's people, for God's people and the church. This will not be an ordinary person, but one who will possess special gifts necessary for our times.

A SEE-ER

The prophet will possess a vision of the times. He or she will be able to see through the spiritual fog and below the surface of things. He will be able to work outside the box and break through walls and barriers of resistance.

The wise man said, *"Where there is no vision, the people perish"* (Proverbs 29:18, KJV). Not only are the people of God perishing, and languishing without sight or knowledge of our times, but they have become caught up and immersed in turmoil. As Malcolm Muggeridge quoted William Blake, "We ever must believe a lie/When we see with, not through, the eye."[6] Consider what William Blake saw in a grain of sand, what Coleridge saw in a seagull, what Handel saw in the book of Job, what Isaiah saw in the death of a king, or what Jesus saw in a mustard seed.

But what the prophet sees may not be a comfortable message for others to receive. There will be jealousy and envy and hatred by those who cannot see as far, or at all.

It will not be his fault, for he does not seek acceptance or rejection, but only to deliver the message faithfully.

A KNOWER

The prophet or person of God knows some things that must be passed on as a message from God. A prophet knows the triune God. The Father is his creator and sovereign. Jesus is his Saviour and Lord. The Holy Spirit is his anointer, comforter, and guide. He will also know his times and be able to discern what needs to be done. This may come by gift, intuition, study, or prayer and meditation, but all by the motivation and burden of the Holy Spirit that moves the sensitive soul to seek the Lord while he may be found and to call upon him while he is near. He will also know the Scriptures or Word of God, which is living and active, sharper than any two-edged sword, piercing and judging the thoughts and intentions of the heart. And the authority of the prophet will be "Thus says the Lord!"

A TELLER

The mandate of the prophet is to deliver a message from God to God's people.

The message must be told clearly, without compromise, or condition. When God appointed Jeremiah as his prophet in Israel's troubled times, he did three things for him. He anointed him. *"Then the Lord put out his hand and touched my mouth; and the Lord said to me, 'Now I have put my words in your mouth'"* (Jeremiah 1:9).

The Lord appointed him. *"See, today I appoint you over nations and over kingdoms, to pluck up and to pull down, to destroy and to overthrow, to build and to plant"* (Jeremiah 1:10).

The Lord also admonished him. *"But you, gird up your loins; stand up and tell them everything that I command you. Do not break down before them, or I will break you before them. And I for my part have made you today a fortified city, an iron pillar, and a bronze wall, against the whole land... They will fight against you; but they shall not prevail against you, for I am with you, says the Lord, to deliver you"* (Jeremiah 1:17-19).

Today's need is for a prophet to be a see-er, a knower, and a teller.

A FEELER

But the prophet is also a feeler in the sense that there is emotion, involvement, and empathy with those to whom he or she is sent to minister. They come from the people and sit with the people in their need and even their sin. They mourn and grieve, and rejoice and praise. They feel after God and feel after his people. As Ezekiel said of his experience,

> The spirit lifted me up and bore me away; I went in bitterness in the heat of my spirit, the hand of the Lord being strong upon me. I came to the exiles... And I sat among them, stunned, for seven days. (Ezekiel 3:14-15)

A FAILURE

The prophets often failed in their mission. For Ezekiel, the people were mostly unreceptive. *"But the house of Israel will not listen you, for they are not willing to listen to me; because all the house of Israel have a hard forehead and a stubborn heart"* (Ezekiel 3:7). They were disobedient and hostile to the message of repentance and change. With the pressure and emphasis for success at any cost on the modern pastor, most would-be prophets are already failures by the time they have reached the third year of their first pastorate. They adjust to the status quo and find that the way to get along is to go along.

A FUTURE

Is there a future for a prophet in our day beyond sacrifice, denial, and even spiritual martyrdom in the cause of Christ? The answer is a positive yes and amen! The Lord has not forsaken his people. He has yet a plan a purpose for them. In the promising words of Isaiah:

> Therefore the Lord waits to be gracious to you; therefore he will rise up to show mercy to you. For the Lord is a God of justice; blessed are all those who wait for him… He will surely be gracious to you at the sound of your cry; when he hears it, he will answer you… And when you turn to the right or when you turn to the left, your ears shall hear a word behind you, saying, "This is the way; walk in it." (Isaiah 30:18-19, 20)

SEVEN

The Jesus Life

From the book *Chris Tomlin: The Way I Was Made, Words and Music for an Unusual Life* comes the thought of the Jesus Life. Paul's letter to the Philippians outlines the wonderful humility of Christ.

> Let the same mind be in you that was in Christ Jesus, who, though he was in the form of God, did not regard equality with God as something to be exploited, but emptied himself, taking the form of a slave, being born in human likeness. And being found in human form, he humbled himself and became obedient to the point of death—even death on a cross (Philippians 2:5-8).

Chris, as a contemporary songwriter and worship leader, gives three important insights into Jesus' life from this text and seeks to apply them to contemporary Christians.

Unnoticed—Jesus was unnoticed from age twelve in the temple to age thirty in Nazareth when his three-year ministry began. This was God's purpose for him so that he could grow and mature without interference or notice from the surrounding and probing world.

Obscure—Jesus came from obscurity to prominence. Once his hand was revealed, he had nowhere to hide, little time to himself, and was under constant pressure and scrutiny. As Thomas A. Kempis observed,

> The greatest saints shunned the company of men when they could, and chose rather to live to God in secret. There was one who said: As often as I have been amongst men, I have returned home less a man … No man can safely appear in public but who loves seclusion.[7]

Jesus did this for eighteen years before beginning his ministry and often sought obscurity during the three years of his public work.

Chris Tomlin's friend and mentor, "J.D.," wrote some lyrics about this:

> Lord, make me obscure
> Keep me unnoticed
> Let me be known by Your image in me

Broken by grace and mended by mercy
Let me be hidden
Hidden in You[8]

Unfamous—Fame does strange things to people, often
making them other than they are or really want to be. There
is an insatiable desire to know what is going on in other peo-
ples' lives, as if our own are so boring and uninteresting that
we must vicariously experience life through others. Jesus did
not want that for himself or for us, often escaping the papa-
razzi of his day.

Tomlin used a thought from one of his band members to
emphasize this. They wore and passed out T-shirts at concerts with a simple star on the front with the words written
across it, "I am not famous." They went like hotcakes!

A friend of Chris' who played for Shania Twain's band
wore one of the t-shirts at one of her concerts in front of millions on TV.

Other words could be gleaned from this text to describe
what Christians and followers of Jesus in every age ought to
be like.

Humble—This was the whole tenor of Jesus' life. He set
aside deity, eternity, and all that comes with it. He "emptied
himself of all but love," as a hymn describes it.[9] Some may
have theological questions about this "emptying," but it simply means that in Jesus, God became one of us in all that hu-
manness could possibly mean.

Non-grasping—Paul admonishes, *Do nothing from self-
ish ambition or conceit*" (Philippians 2:3). This goes against

everything that western civilization and culture screams at us from birth to the end of life. But Jesus had nothing to grasp after or to attain. He had it all and willingly set it aside.

Non-attitude—This means there is nothing to prove. As Paul said, *"regard others as better than yourselves"* (Philippians 2:3). Gone is the need to prove oneself to another by some kind of display, feat, or competition. We already acknowledge that they have won and are better! We gladly take second place. Jesus, in a sense, took last place, even though he was born for first and in the end will claim it and be given it by his Father.

Non-interest—*"Let each of you look not to your own interests, but to the interests of others"* (Philippians 2:4). This "non-interest" is an old Puritan and mystical term meaning a passive response to God, a "let go and let God" approach. Jesus seemed to float along in his approach to this life of non-interest and centeredness in his Father.

Obedient—Jesus always did the right thing as his Father desired and asked of him. There were no slips, no failings, and no folly on the road to doing the will of God.

Only once in the Garden of Gethsemane was there even an appearance of an almost giving in, but that was not to resist the will of God, but to confirm it.

Cross-conscious—The end of Jesus' life on earth was on a cross. It was cruel, uncompromising, and deadly. No one can die like he did. Jesus did not star in his own show. He was a spectacle, a sacrifice pinned to a tree, hanging for all to see. He calls everyone as a follower to carry his or her own cross daily. And our cross is not a cross of wood with nails in our hands and feet. It is the price anyone pays to be obedient to Jesus in every way.

Death willing—Jesus willingly died for us. We are called to be willing for death, too, if required. And if we are not willing, we can be willing to be made willing by his Holy Spirit's pleading, prodding and praying that we might be conformed to Christ, and *"be of the same mind, having the same love, being in full accord and of one mind"* (Philippians 2:2).

But this death is not a self-crucifixion; it is the work of God, as in Romans 6:6-12 and 12:1-2, or as in *"I have been crucified with Christ; and it is no longer I who live, but it is Christ who lives in me"* (Galatians 2:19-20).

This death is a spiritual, internal privation of the soul experienced as a crisis or as a continuous and conscious identification with Jesus, and a rising to new life and victory in Christ.

EIGHT

Doesn't God See?

The church is in a mess. Doesn't God see it?

Listen to the litany of issues at a typical local church. At the last church business meeting, the renovation of the nursery was torpedoed again. The Pastoral Search Committee can't decide which of its two prime candidates to recommend to the congregation as their new pastor, and another chairman has resigned. A key financial supporter has asked that his automatic withdrawal of offerings be cancelled. An outside worship team has finally been allowed to play in one service this summer, but under strict conditions. The issue could be anything from the use of the building, the youth, the worship committee, the preaching, or anything else… but it seems that things are falling apart in the church, and doesn't God see?

The Bible tells us that we are to agree, that there should be peace among God's people, that unity and oneness should characterize our meetings, but doesn't God see? The cry is, "We are falling apart! People are leaving and no one new is taking their place!"

With everything that is happening, our direction is missing, our growth has been stunted, we are reinventing the wheel over and over, and the blessing is passing us by for someone or some group who has their focus straight, their issues resolved, and God and his glory in view. What has happened to us?

Have we been too blind, too deaf, too self-absorbed to see and hear and understand what the Lord Jesus is trying to do with his church?

The early church had the agreement and consensus of their leadership to move ahead in their decision about the inclusion of the new Gentile believers. Is Woody Allen right when he said, "If Jesus returned today and saw what people were doing in his name he wouldn't stop throwing up."[10] Is the enemy short circuiting us and leading us in a circle? Are we out of step with the Holy Spirit and what the Lord Jesus wants to do with us?

Isaiah has some good advice for the church of our day. *"Therefore the Lord waits to be gracious to you; therefore he will rise up to show mercy to you. For the Lord is a God of justice; blessed are all who wait for him"* (Isaiah 30:18).

The letters to the churches in Revelation 2-3 tell us that Jesus has a word to say to the church then and now. It is a word of forsaking the first love (Ephesus), slander and suffering (Smyrna), belief and behaviour (Pergamum), tolerating immorality (Thyatira), spiritual lethargy (Sardis), love and faithfulness (Philadelphia), and lukewarm and compromised (Laodicea). Unless we relegate these figures of churches to a future dispensation, or make them a product of a past or future historical timeframe no longer relevant, their message is universal and applicable today.

In every day and generation, there is something wrong with the church that the Lord of the church takes issue with and wants to correct. Only the church in Philadelphia had a totally positive record. So there must be some form of it visible right now and today.

God does see what is happening with his church today and is concerned as some of his servants are in alarming numbers as they cry for help. The church is on fire and there is nothing to put it out. But God surely sees it first. The question is, why can't we get along without going along with every passing craze, fade, or fashion? What is wrong with *"it has seemed good to the Holy Spirit and to us"* (Acts 15:28), in deciding touchy issues and change in the church?

Jesus as the Lord of the church does cares about his body, his building, and his bride. He is watching her growth, grooming and groaning for his return. Why would Jesus give his life for the church and not be interested in what is happening to it? The answer is that he is! Jesus, by his Holy Spirit, is discipling his church in various ways. As the writer to the Hebrews reminds us, *"For the Lord disciplines those [churches] whom he loves, and chastises every child [church] whom he accepts"* (Hebrews 12:6).

Perhaps one answer is the same as when Israel was delivered from the Egyptians in the Red Sea and rejoiced.

> But they soon forgot his works; they did not wait for his counsel. But they had a wanton craving in the wilderness, and put God to the test in the desert; he gave them what they asked, but sent a wasting disease among them. (Psalm 106:13-15)

They were ultimately sent into captivity twice before returning to the land to rebuild. The prophets told them to expect a redeemer and Messiah. But when he came as Jesus at Bethlehem, John tells us that the world did not know him and his own did not accept him (John 1:10-11). Even when facing the cross, Jesus lamented the unbelief of the Jews in the prophetic words:

> Jerusalem, Jerusalem, the city that kills the prophets and stones those who are sent to it! How often have I desired to gather your children together as a hen gathers her brood under her wings, and you were not willing! See, your house is left to you, desolate. For I tell you, you will not see me again until you say, 'Blessed is the one who comes in the name of the Lord.' (Matthew 23:37-39)

As a nation, historically, the Jews still have not accepted Jesus as their Messiah. But Romans 9-11 is their great hope and future, and should be the burdened prayer of every child of God.

But the question for the Gentile, or other churches, is whether they can be set aside in the same way through disobedience and unbelief? They would surely say no, but doesn't God see?

Most church growth or church health experts say that the western church has a limited time to change and move into the twenty-first century with her message and ministry, before it falls into a flatline. Many of the present generation believe this has already happened for them, as they seek alternate forms of worship or expressions of their spirituality. But, doesn't God see?

NINE

Holy Sweat

There is an understood axiom of Christian ministry that any work or labour done in the name of Christ must be done in the power of the Holy Spirit and not by human sweat. This means that the flesh, the old man, the self is unacceptable as a vessel of God for holy work. The flesh must be denied, counted as dead, and crucified with the life, walk, and work now done in the Holy Spirit. As the progressive refrain of an old hymn expresses it:

> All of self and none of Thee,
> Some of self and some of Thee,
> Less of self and more of Thee,
> None of self and all of Thee.[11]

The last line is the desire and goal of the Christian servant of God—"None of self and all of Thee." If we accept this as being true and the will of God, there seems yet to be a place for holy sweat, or the working up of the holy within us to the point of perspiring or sweating for God. This is found in the theme of Jesus' twin parables on prayer in Luke 11 and 18. In the first, the man at midnight, coming to his friend for bread on behalf of another, perseveres and is persistent to the point of shame and annoyance before he gets what he wants. Jesus' follow-up teaching is: ask and receive, seek and find, knock and the door will be opened.

The key lesson is that God the Father will give the Holy Spirit to those who ask him as the means of getting what is natural and appropriate—food, gifts, anything. There seems to be work and effort and sweat in this, but it is holy sweat.

Similarly, Luke 18 tells of an unjust judge who is persuaded by a widow to give her justice because, even though he has no fear of God or respect for anyone, her bothering and continual coming might wear him out. Jesus indicates that this is the way to get answers to prayer from God for those who *"cry to him day and night"* (18:7) and *"pray always and… [do] not lose heart"* (18:1). This likewise seems to be effort, and sweaty work. But it is holy and acceptable because God is in it and even sanctions the process. Is the modern church and Christian servant of God missing something here?

As poet John Milton said about seeking and inquiry, in 1644,

> I cannot praise a fugitive and cloistered vir-
> tue, unexercised and unbreathed, that never
> sallies out and sees her adversary, but slinks
> out of the race, where the immortal garland
> is to be run for, not without dust and heat.[12]

Paul said he worked harder than anyone else in the kingdom, but it was not he, but the grace of God. As he assured
the Galatians, *"I have been crucified with Christ; and it is no
longer I who live, but it is Christ who lives in me. And the life I
now live in the flesh I live by faith of the Son of God, who loved
me and gave himself for me"* (Galatians 2:19-20).

This same effort and holy sweat seemed to motivate the
prayer of Jacob (Genesis 32:22-32) and the prayer of Jabez
(1 Chronicles 4:9-10). Is it time to work up a holy sweat?

TEN

The Wicked in Worship

A strange and dangerous trend is being seen in church work and worship. Non-Christians, unbelievers, atheists, and even "the wicked" are showing up in places of leadership. This is how it is happening.

Some churches short on members to volunteer for leadership positions now accept non-members to certain boards and committees. With the openings, few if any questions are asked about spiritual life or commitment to Christ. Once in places of leadership, it is possible to pass on thoughts, ideas, plans, programs, and actions that are directly or indirectly at cross-purposes or even dangerous for the local church to take, let alone against the will of God.

It is reported that the college of organists in the United States has issued a directive that churches seeking and interviewing candidates can no longer ask them if they are Christian. Could this move be extended to the Pastoral Search Committee when they can no longer ask if the pastoral candidate is a Christian?

Worship teams in some mega churches often accept non-Christian musicians as staff members or worship participants as long as they go along with the team's philosophy of ministry.

What is happening here? Is the Lord and his work so hard up for workers and bodies that anyone, even non-Christians and "the wicked," is acceptable? God says this should not be.

> But to the wicked God says: "What right have you to recite my statutes, or take my covenant on your lips? For you hate discipline, and you cast my words behind you... You give your mouth free rein for evil, and your tongue frames deceit... These things you have done and I have been silent; you thought that I was one just like yourself. But now I rebuke you, and lay the charge before you. (Psalm 50:16-17, 19, 21)

In summary, God says, the wicked (unbelievers) have no rights. They are not qualified spiritually. Their lives are not pleasing to God. They think that God doesn't care. They believe that God will do nothing about it, because he is just like them. They are wrong!

There is likewise a New Testament warning, in which Paul says:

> Do not be mismatched with unbelievers. For what partnership is there between righteousness and lawlessness? Or what fellowship is there between light and darkness? What agreement does Christ have with Beliar [the Devil]? Or what does a believer share with an unbeliever? What agreement has the temple of God with idols? (2 Corinthians 6:14-16)

God's answer to the unbeliever, non-Christian, or even the wicked person in Christian work or ministry must be, "God doesn't want you or need you to serve him."

It is an affront and scandal to God that anyone should presume to take upon them a holy task because they are willing and some well-meaning person has asked them. God is holy and requires holy ones to worship and to serve him. This is the whole idea of a separated person, called of God to serve him. Come out from among them and be blessed as you serve the Lord.

ELEVEN

Vows for Spiritual Power

The wise man Solomon said, *"When you make a vow to God, do not delay fulfilling it; for he has no pleasure in fools. Fulfill what you vow"* (Ecclesiastes 5:4). Jesus said, *"Let your word be 'Yes, Yes' or 'No, No'"* (Matthew 5:37). There are good vows we can offer to God, and bad vows or promises which we should not offer or speak to God.

Here are six vows made to God shortly after the calling to the ministry, which have been followed by the author for over forty years to great profit, power, and blessing. This followed the experience of the fullness of the Holy Spirit with the assurance of being called to preach the gospel with an affirming witness. *"He has made known to us the mystery of his will, according to his good pleasure that he set forth in Christ"* (Ephesians 1:9).

GIVE GOD THE GLORY

"He must increase, but I must decrease" (John 3:30).

In all things relating to the Christian life and ministry, God must receive the glory. That is, God must get the honour and respect, have first place, get the fame, and receive the worship and praise. As John the Baptist's ministry declined when Jesus arrived on the scene, so the servant of the Lord recedes into the background as the Lord Jesus is lifted up, preached and proclaimed.

It should be a natural progression for others to see Christ instead of the servant, the contents instead of the vessel carrying it, to smell the fragrance of the Holy Spirit, and to feel the liberty and freedom he brings.

KNOW BY EXPERIENCE THE DEEPER LIFE TRUTHS

"I believed, and so I spoke" (2 Corinthians 4:13).

A servant can only speak from his or her own personal spiritual experience of what God has done for them and through them. It is crucial to believe the right things in the orthodox Christian tradition and to speak them consistently to the people of God. To do this brings assurance, authority, credibility, and conviction to what is said or preached. When we say, "Thus says the Lord," in word or in tone, it has impact and results in moving the hearers to acknowledge that the Lord is among them. There is no place for dead or dull orthodoxy.

KEEP HUMBLE AND MEEK

"Humble yourselves therefore under the mighty hand of God, so that he may exalt you in due time" (1 Peter 5:6).

This means being nothing in self and everything in Christ. It is a deliberate preaching of the Word with Paul's words in heart and mind:

> When I came to you, brothers and sisters, I did not come proclaiming the mystery of God to you in lofty words of wisdom. For I decided to know nothing among you except Jesus Christ, and him crucified. And I came to you in weakness and in fear and in much trembling. My speech and my proclamation were not with plausible words of wisdom, but with a demonstration of the Spirit and of power, so that your faith might rest not on human wisdom but on the power of God. (1 Corinthians 2:1-5)

REALIZE YOUR LIMITATIONS

"He is able to deal gently with the ignorant and wayward, since he himself is subject to weakness" (Hebrews 5:2). *"For he knows how we were made; he remembers that we are dust"* (Psalm 103:14).

The servant of God is weak in the flesh and can only do so much before the constitution begins to suffer and break down. Not only do we have limited energy, time and place, but in identifying with the people to whom we minister, we carry the same gene and are able to feel and to empathize with their sins, sorrows, ignorance, and waywardness. As the apostle John counselled Gaius, *"Beloved, I pray that all may go well with you and that you may be in good health, just as it is well with you soul"* (3 John 1:2).

It can be said as an axiom for those serving others: Anyone wanting to save, heal, feed, and strengthen others must themselves be saved, healed, fed, and strengthened. As Paul counselled young Timothy in his leadership, *"Pay close attention to yourself and to your teaching; continue in these things, for in doing this you will save both yourself and your hearers"* (1 Timothy 4:16). A bleeding heart is no good if it bleeds to death, unless you are the Messiah, and there was only one!

IN ALL THINGS IS LOVE THE MOTIVE?

"[If I] do not have love, I am nothing" (1 Corinthians 13:2).

Loving God, and loving our neighbours as ourselves, is the key to ministry. If we lose this, we are lost and forlorn. The servant must constantly examine his heart to determine that love is the key motive for ministry. It will carry him far and keep him faithful in the service of Christ.

MAKE THE WORD CENTRAL IN PREACHING

"As the Lord lives, whatever the Lord says to me, that I will speak" (1 Kings 22:14). *"I could not go beyond the command of the Lord my God, to do less or more"* (Numbers 22:18).

We dare not get caught up in the passing fancies of the world in our preaching. Not that we are not to be relevant and up to date in matters of history, culture, economics, and political changes. But we must critique them by the Word of God, and judge them accordingly, and not in the reverse.

TWELVE
Holy Anger

God got angry, and so did Jesus. Moses expressed anger, as did the apostle Paul. So what is so bad about losing your temper and getting angry? Every parent knows what it means to lose control temporarily to express displeasure and anger, even toward their favourite child. Everyone feels bad and guilty about getting angry, even if we can justify it. It is something that our conscience just won't let go of. Who has the right to be angry and who does not?

We would probably all agree that God has the right to be angry at sin and to punish it as he sees fit. We would also agree that if he has set down standards by which we humans are to live under his sovereignty, then he has the right to require behaviour in line with those laws, rules, and expectations.

We might also agree that Jesus Christ the Lord showed his anger and distain for sin's abuse when he cast the money-changers out of the temple with a scourge. Peter must certainly have been frustrated and angry when challenged with knowing Jesus at one of his trials. He clearly cursed at the time. Paul cursed the high priest who was trying to find fault in his testimony about Jesus and then apologized for breaking the law in so doing.

But with all of the above in mind, Paul instructs the Ephesian Christians, *"Be angry but do not sin; do not let the sun go down on your anger, and do not make room for the devil."* (Ephesians 4:26-27).

There seems to be an important truth here about anger, which every seeking Christian ought to consider. There are both positive and negative sides.

The passage refers to individual and personal anger. Everyone gets angry, even mature Christians. There is an anger which is after godliness and not sinful. We call it righteous indignation. There is a time limit on carrying angry feelings and allowing them to fester, seethe, and take control of the mind and heart and to disturb our peace. The enemy of our souls uses anger as a lever into our spirits. A day is the time limit for anger. Anger is not to result in personal revenge or payback. Forgiveness, confession, reconciliation, and restoration are the norms.

Dr. Samuel Johnson, the eighteenth century writer said to be the father of the English dictionary,[13] when asked to water down some of the strong language in his writings, said,

"He would not cut off his claws, nor make his tiger a cat to please anybody."[14]

John Wesley said, "Give me a hundred men who fear nothing but God, and who hate nothing but sin, and who know nothing but Jesus Christ and him crucified, and I will shake the world."[15]

As one commentator suggests, "The Christian must be sure that his anger is that of righteous indignation, and not just an expression of personal provocation or wounded pride. It must have no sinful motives, nor be allowed to lead to sin in any way."[16] On the other hand, John Stott tells us, "…there is a great need in the contemporary world for more Christian anger. We human beings compromise with sin in a way in which God never does. In the face of blatant evil we should be indignant not tolerant, angry not apathetic. If God hates sin, his people should hate it too. If evil arouses his anger, it should arouse ours too."[17]

It says of Jesus, "You have loved righteousness and hated wickedness; therefore God, your God, has anointed you with the oil of gladness beyond your companions" (Hebrews 1:9, Psalm 45:7). Should this not also be true of his followers?

As the prophet Isaiah pronounced,

> Ah, you who call evil good, and good evil, who put darkness for light and light for darkness, who put bitter for sweet, and sweet for bitter! (Isaiah 5:20)

There is a price to pay for just letting things go. Anger at abuse and evil human behaviour is both biblical and the morally right thing to do. As we are reminded by British philosopher Edmund Burke, "The only thing necessary for the triumph of evil is for good men to do nothing."[18] Holy anger is from God. When men are angry in a holy cause, God is in it. If God cannot be in it, it is unholy and evil and the Christian must say NO!

THIRTEEN

The Discipline of the Servant

Discipleship begins after you believe. When a Christian says "I do" to Christ, the honeymoon of belief gives way to the daily routine of the Christian life. Jesus talked about the cost of it in Luke 14:25-33. From this, we can learn several good lessons about following as a servant and a leader.

DISCIPLESHIP IS NOT A MASS MOVEMENT

Jesus was enjoying great box-office appeal. He was performing miracles, healing, and telling stories in parables. As a result, large crowds were following him. He wanted to weed out the true disciples from the hangers on and challenged them, *"Whoever comes to me and does not hate father and mother, wife and children, brother and sisters, yes, and even life itself, cannot be my disciple"* (Luke 14:26).

He made this challenge at another time, but *"because of this many of his disciples turned back and no longer went about with him"* (John 6:66). He gave them a cause for pause. He wanted them to avoid a Palm Sunday parade that was going to end up in a Good Friday crucifixion. What kind of people considered following?

Speculators—These dabbled and were in and out of things quickly. They had been scratched by Christianity but not infected by it.

They had been warmed by the teachings of Jesus, enjoyed his company, liked his manner and gentleness, but when the going got tough, they disappeared. They were looking for needs to be met now, not for a price to be paid at the checkout counter.

Spectators—These are the more serious types. They will join, get involved, make friends, and enjoy the rites of passage in the church; that is, hatched, matched and dispatched (births, weddings, funerals). They will give a little, serve a little, cheer success and applaud a winner, but when trouble comes or there is a losing streak, the call is "fire the coach!" (Or the pastor.)

Censorious—These are the hardened church members who have been around a long time and couldn't be moved with a stick of dynamite. They are the "don't like" crowd. They don't like changes—the noise of children, young people roughhousing, the pastor who doesn't visit enough, programs that focus on other "outside" people. It is like the letter of complaint to the editor of a religious magazine:

> I am deeply distressed by your magazine. There hasn't been a publication whose theological treatises I've been so offended by, whose candid accounts of bickering among churches I've been so embarrassed by, whose nagging reminders of the needs of the world and church I've been made to feel so guilty by since – well, since the New Testament.[19]

DISCIPLESHIP MEANS CHOICES

Jesus was calling those who would follow him to make some tough choices in their lives.

Family—*"Whoever comes to me and does not hate his father and mother, wife and children, brothers and sisters, yes, and even life itself, cannot be my disciple"* (Luke 14:26). To "hate" means here "to love more than." Jesus is calling for the choice of him above any domestic or family tie or bond. This is a tough choice for many. It's like leaving everything and immigrating to a new country. It's like joining the armed forces to fight for one's country against a foreign enemy. It's the choice of saying no and goodbye to all!

Jesus wanted them to know that at the end of the road for him and any who followed was a cross and death as far as this worldly life was concerned.

Familiar—*"Hate... even life itself"* meant the choice of the familiar—our desires, feelings, goals, and plans that might get in the way of God's will and purpose for us. This means there are to be no "keep out" signs or "hands off" warnings on our lives to stop God the Holy Spirit from intruding and inspecting, and possibly excluding, whatever might be offensive to him or the cause of Christ. This all or nothing choice and commitment is too demanding for some, and Jesus allowed many to walk away from it.

Foolish—*"Whoever does not carry the cross and follow me cannot be my disciple"* (Luke 14:27). This may sound like a foolish choice for some. But the cross the disciple is called to carry is not a piece of jewellery around the neck, nor a wooden symbol in a church, nor a personal weakness or frailty we might say is "my cross to bear." It is our deliberate identification with Christ, which brings whatever rebuke, suffering, losses, pain, abuse or sorrow our way because we believe in and belong to Christ by faith and commitment.

Practically, this means that Jesus' suffering is our suffering. Jesus' rejection is our rejection. Jesus' wounds are our wounds. Jesus' death is our death. Jesus' cross is our cross. Jesus' shame is our shame.

In the fatal words of Dietrich Bonhoeffer, "When Christ calls a man, he bids him come and die."[20]

A.W. Tozer gave an illustration of the cost of discipleship as a threefold view of a man on the cross. "The man who is crucified is facing only one direction. He cannot look back... he has no further plans of his own. Someone else made his plans for him, and when they nailed him up there all his plans disappeared... when you go out to die on the cross you bid goodbye... you are not going back!"[21]

DISCIPLESHIP IS COSTLY

Jesus gave two examples of the cost of discipleship. One was of someone building a tower, and the other was of someone planning for a war. Each must plan, estimate costs, take into account risks and expectations of completion, and of victory or defeat. The true follower of Jesus should do this, be willing to follow through to the end and to put up the necessary proofs of intent. David Watson gives us a list of questions to be asked of a young disciple of Jesus: Are they willing to serve? Are they able to listen? Are they willing to learn? Can they take correction? Can they submit to others over themselves and live with others? Are they able to examine their own lives, know their own weaknesses and strengths? Are they perfectionists? Can they forgive, stick it out, be trusted, keep confidences and do little things well?[22]

In building, there are options, choices, planning. It is more of a passive preparation. In war, the battle is brought to you, and you either engage or entreat and come to terms.

The implication is that one must be ready and prepared with no reservations or questions unresolved. The results are that costly!

Everything may not be required, but everything must be offered. Not all are on the front lines, but all must be on duty to serve, even on the sidelines to cheer. As someone has said by way of commitment, "If not you, who? If not here, where? If not now, when?"

FOURTEEN

Dreamers for God

J esus made a startling revelation of who he was to his disciples (see Matthew 16:13-20). His claim was that he was not an incarnation of one of the giants of the faith such as John the Baptist, Elijah, Jeremiah, or one of the prophets. But as Peter answered, "You are the Messiah, the Son of the living God" (Matthew 16:16). From the perspective of what this means for the church and the Christian of any century since, let us dream of some of the possibilities as answers to these questions:

IF JESUS IS THE SON OF GOD—WHAT CAN'T WE DO?

If we assume that what Jesus pronounced is true, there should not be and cannot be any limit to what he can do or his church and people can do in his name. If we add his Great

Commission to this revelation of Jesus as the Son of God, the conclusions are without limit.

> All authority in heaven and on earth has been given to me. Go therefore and make disciples of all nations, baptizing them in the name of the Father and of the Son and of the Holy Spirit, and teaching them to obey everything that I have commanded you. And remember, I am with you always, to the end of the age. (Matthew 28:18-20)

As added encouragement, the following words should strengthen our resolve:

> The one who believes in me will also do the works that I do and, in fact, will do greater works than these, because I am going to the Father. I will do whatever you ask in my name... If in my name you ask me for anything, I will do it. (John 14:12-14)

The church in every generation has always been hampered by her reluctance to step out and claim and do what has been promised. With the lack of results, we end up apologizing and begin to adjust and reinterpret what Jesus said to our shame and the enemy's delight.

IF JESUS IS BUILDING HIS CHURCH—CAN'T WE HELP?

God has made his people and his church co-workers and co-builders, with his Holy Spirit working through us. In a real sense, he has no one else chosen and marked out to do this work. We are the ones who need to be willing, obedient, and faithful to our heavenly calling. With God, one is a majority. We can do all things through Christ who strengthens us. Nothing can separate us from the love of Christ. He has given gifts to his church for the building up of the body. The answer is, we can help and should be a part of the divine building project of spiritual church construction. Without him we cannot, but without us he will not!

IF THE GATES OF HELL CAN'T PREVAIL
AGAINST THE CHURCH—WHAT CAN?

The church seems to suffer from a perpetual hound dog, kicked puppy, defeatist attitude when it comes to doing battle with spiritual forces opposed to her.

Many think losing a battle is the same as losing the war. This is not Jesus' way or will! Continual and constant spiritual battles are fought with the enemy by the church and the people of God. Paul told us that this is normal (see Ephesians 6:10-18). There is not one negative in his words about defeat and loss and retreat. It is, "be strong," "put on," "stand against," "take up," "withstand," "stand firm," "be ready to proclaim," "quench all flaming arrows of the evil one," "take," and "pray." The truth is that nothing on earth, nothing above or below it, can finally and fully prevail or prevent the church from fulfilling its mandate. We need to believe this.

IF THE CHURCH AND CHRISTIANS HAVE BEEN GIVEN THE KEYS TO THE KINGDOM—WHAT CAN'T BE OPENED, AND WHAT CAN CLOSE US DOWN?

This truth has largely been reserved for a small part of the church and not counted as authoritative by most of Protestantism. But this must be revived and acted upon in the daily life of the church when facing opposition, evil, and movements that threaten the health and spiritual progress of the local church. If we can open and close, the prayer life of the church and her spiritual pronouncements are keys to doing the will of God and building the church of Jesus Christ in every generation or place, and nothing and no one can stop what God wants to do in us and through us and to the world.

IF WE HAVE THE POWER TO LOOSE AND TO BIND IN HEAVEN AND ON EARTH—IS ANYTHING IMPOSSIBLE TO US?

This speaks of spiritual power to be enacted on behalf of the health and growth of the church. It is not only the power of excommunication from the church, but exclusion from heaven. Who can have this power but God? Yet Jesus has given to the church this sacred responsibility to be used with great humility, discernment, wisdom, and love in exercising the will of God.

Jesus challenged the disciples with the need for a mustard seed of faith to win the spiritual battle:

> For truly I tell you, if you have faith the size of a mustard seed, you will say to this mountain, "Move from here to there," and it will move; and nothing will be impossible for you. (Matthew 17:20)

IF JESUS PROMISED IT—WHY CAN'T WE CLAIM IT?

Some may have gone too far in claiming what has not been the will of God or the plan of Jesus. But there is something in this section of God's Word which could unleash great power in the church and society for God and for good. Is it possible to ask for and claim the renewal, revival, and restoration of the church of our day and any day for Christ? Is it worth a try? Can we not be dreamers for God?

FIFTEEN

What Is a Christian? Part I

A church bulletin had printed this as its creed or belief system:

On the Holy Trinity, I am a Catholic.
On esteem for the Bible as God's Word, I am Brethren
On justification by faith, I am Lutheran
On holiness, I am Methodist
On assurance, I am Reformed
On water baptism, I am Baptist
On worship, I am charismatic
On the Holy Spirit, I am Pentecostal
On concern for the hurting, I am Salvation Army
On our Master's Great Commission, I am Alliance

This seems to cover all the bases of belief. Or does it?

All of these denominational representatives or groups would call themselves Christian. But there is little definition of what a Christian really is. The New Testament begins with four gospels, or books, about the life and ministry of Jesus. But there is no description or definition of what a Christian is until you get to The Acts of the Apostles and the other letters.

The word or name Christian is mentioned only three times in the New Testament, and each context or incident of its use helps us to understand the question, "What is a Christian?" Let us consider the first reference.

"And it was in Antioch that the disciples were first called "Christians" (Acts 11:26).

The church was founded in Jerusalem, but the believers were called "believers," "disciples," "saints," "any who belonged to the Way" (Acts 9:2), or "brothers" (9:17). But this is the first time there is a reference to a Christian. The reason they were called Christians first at Antioch was because there was evidence of a change in their lives. It was a dramatic change, a life-changing change, an identifying change that made them called "Christ-ones," or Christians.

The first believers or converts to Christ in Jerusalem were Jews who still practiced as Jews but had added belief in Jesus as their Christ or Messiah. Today they would call themselves "completed Jews." But in Antioch, there was a Greek population and any who wanted to worship God did so as a proselyte or convert to Judaism. But there was something very special and significant that happened in Antioch to designate a brand new word to describe it—"Christian."

> But among them were some men of Cyprus and Cyrene who, on coming to Antioch, spoke to the Hellenists also, proclaiming the Lord Jesus. The hand of the Lord was with them, and a great number became believers and turned to the Lord. (Acts 11:20-21)

The church at Jerusalem heard of this. They sent Barnabas. He went and got Paul. They both spent a whole year with the church and taught a great number of people. So marked was the change—in individuals, families, communities, commerce, and politics—that they came to be called "Christians!"

WHAT THE AVERAGE PERSON MIGHT SAY

When asked if they're a Christian, the average person today might say, "Of course I'm a Christian. I was born in a Christian country. What do you think I am, a heathen? I was raised in a Christian church. I was baptized (christened). My parents made me go and get it done, you know, dunked. I try to keep the Ten Commandments and the Sermon on the Mount. Isn't that what they call it? You know, the ten "Thou shalt not's" and the "blessed this, blessed that" eight times. We're all Christians, aren't we?"

What do you think about this question? There used to be a question regarding a Christian witness, "If you were arrested for being a Christian, would there be enough evidence to convict you?" Would there be? Has there been enough change in our lives to be designated "Christian?"

WHAT WE ARE TO CONSIDER BY EXAMPLE

George Whitefield was a great preacher and evangelist of eighteenth century England. But first, he was an Anglican minister and a missionary to the natives of the new colonies in America. He belonged to a Holy Club along with the Wesley brothers, John and Charles. But he was not yet a Christian. On February 23, 1736, George began to read a little book lent to him by Charles Wesley called *The Life of God in the Soul of Man*, by Henry Scougal. He wrote,

> I had fasted, watched, prayed, received the sacrament, but read that true religion is not in these outward things, 'religion was the union of the soul with God, and Christ formed within us,' a ray of divine light was instantaneously darted in upon my soul, and from that moment, but not till then, did I know that I must be a new creature.[23]

Consider the following examples:

Paul said, *"God chose to make known how great among the Gentiles are the riches of the glory of this mystery, which is Christ in you, the hope of glory"* (Colossians 1:27).

Jesus said to Nicodemus, a religious leader of the Jews, *"You must be born from above [born again]"* (John 3:7). This is not a womb birth, a will birth, or a water birth, but a wind birth, of the Spirit, from above, born of God (John 1:13). Jesus was saying, "Nicodemus, God must come upon you and change you."

Charles Colson was legal counsel to President Richard Nixon and was being prosecuted for his involvement in the Watergate break-ins of April and May 1972 in the United States. He was reading C.S. Lewis' *Mere Christianity*, given to him by a friend about change.

He knew he was heading for jail, but there in his car, in tears, he was "born again." He wrote a book about it and called it *Born Again.*

Augustine was a sensual young man in the fourth century A.D. He had both a wife and a mistress. He could not control his sexual appetites until he was led to read from the New Testament book of Romans:

> Let us live honorably, as in the day, not in reveling and drunkenness, not in debauchery and licentiousness, not in quarreling and jealousy. Instead, put on the Lord Jesus Christ, and make no provision for the flesh, to gratify its desires. (Romans 13:13-14)

He was changed and became the most influential church father of the ancient world, and even to the modern era.

In the sixteenth century, Martin Luther was a priest and theology professor. He was trying to get right with God by works and a discipline of the flesh until he was led to read, *"The one who is righteous will live by faith"* (Romans 1:17).

He was changed and became the leader of the Protestant Reformation.

Paul, called Saul, was a young aspiring and zealous rabbi contemporary with Jesus. He was rushing to persecute Christians, as he had already witnessed Stephen's martyrdom and consented to it. God smote him to the ground and changed him. He was never the same again (see Acts 9:1-22) He became the most influential Christian and the writer of more New Testament books than any other. As Lord Lyttelton said of him,

> The conversion and apostleship of St. Paul alone, duly considered, was of itself a demonstration sufficient to prove Christianity a divine revelation.[24]

In 1971, John Stott, an Anglican evangelical Bible teacher and chaplain to the Queen, had just published his book, *Basic Christianity*. He got a note from a well-known British preacher, which said,

> Dear John, thank you for writing *Basic Christianity*; it led me to make a new commitment of my life to Christ. I am old now, nearly seventy-eight, but not too old to make a new beginning.
> Signed, Leslie Wetherhead.[25]

CAN WE MAKE THIS PERSONAL?

What do you think? Could someone look at your life and say, "Yes, I see a change in you. I can tell that you are a Christian." Has there been that change?

What does it mean to change and become a Christian? Someone might say, "I've been raised in the church and can't remember a time I didn't believe in God. I accept that Jesus is the Son of God and that he died for me. I've been dedicated as an infant, and baptized or confirmed as a teenager. I have the certificates somewhere. I've become a member of this church and am serving on a committee or Board. What more do I need?"

We are not questioning the process, but we need to be clear. In a Christian and church-saturated culture and society, it is often assumed that the normal processes of initiation makes one a Christian. We have assented to these things, and have not denied them. What is this need for change and commitment to Christ that seems to be in focus here?

Here is the key issue. Aside from what each church practices as its rites of passage into the Christian faith, we must insist on a regenerate church membership. This is one of the basic tenants of the Christian church as outlined in the Bible.

In *The Empty Church: The Suicide of Liberal Christianity*, Thomas Reeves reviewed the historic trend of most mainline churches in America and concluded that the majority of churches have gone from mainline, to oldline, to sideline, and finally to flatline. He claims this has nothing to do with liturgy or worship styles. It is basic teaching, preaching, and the belief system of each church.[26]

As an historical example, he cites John Henry Newman in 1830s England trying to renew the spiritual life of the Anglican Church, who had a picture of Oxford University on the wall in his room with the scripture verse from Ezekiel 37:3 below it, *"Can these [dry] bones live?"*[27]

Put simply, if there has been no discernable change in our lives, can we call ourselves Christians? This is not a criticism against childhood decisions for Christ and baptism or confirmation at a reasonable age, but does it work and do we stick? We should not be hearing this for the first time! Our Sunday Schools should have it as a part of its curriculum. There should be opportunity to respond to this kind of message on a regular basis. We should be able to follow up on people who make such decisions and commitments. We should be able to train people to lead others to faith in Christ apart from an evangelistic crusade. If someone asked you how to become a Christian, could you help him or her to do so?

An older Christian witness used to travel the subway system with a large button on his lapel with a question mark on it. When asked what it meant, he would direct inquirers to Acts 16 and Paul's witness to the Philippian jailer when the jailer asked, *"'Sirs, what must I do to be save?" [Paul and Silas] answered, "Believe on the Lord Jesus, and you will be saved, you and your household"* (Acts 16:30-31). This is the very heart of it!

They were called Christians first at Antioch. Did they call themselves that or did the people watching their lives say, "These people have been with Jesus; they must be Christians!" What is a Christian? It is a changed person!

SIXTEEN

What Is a Christian? Part II

As we think further about the question "What is a Christian?" we consider Paul's defence before King Agrippa. In it, we see that a Christian is someone who makes a choice. *"Agrippa said to Paul, 'Are you so quickly persuading me to become a Christian?'"* (Acts 26:28)

So why should we choose to become a Christian?

BECAUSE OF WHAT JESUS DID

Paul was convinced that some things about Jesus were common knowledge.

Jesus came in fulfillment of the Hebrew Scriptures—the prophets and Moses agreed—Christ would come, would suffer, would rise from the dead, and would be believed on by his own people and the Gentiles.

Thirty years after the events of Calvary and the church's birth (about 60 A.D.), the facts about it were widespread. *"These people who have been turning the world upside down have come here also"* (Acts 17:6). The ruling Roman authorities were aware of it—Felix, Festus, Agrippa, and the Roman court, even Caesar's household had Christians as employees. Listen to what Paul says to Agrippa:

> Indeed the king knows about these things, and to him I speak freely; for I am certain that none of these things has escaped his notice, for this was not done in a corner. King Agrippa, do you believe the prophets? I know that you believe. (Acts 26:26-27)

We could say that after two thousand years, the facts of the gospel are still well known or are at least a part of the culture or religious traditions of most of Western society. Not many can say, "I have never heard of Jesus Christ or what he did in the first century A.D." The younger generation, however, seems to be missing out on the influences of a Christian home, Sunday School, and religious instruction in the school systems.

Why should we choose?

BECAUSE OF WHAT JESUS DEMANDS

Jesus' death and resurrection requires a response or choice from those who consider it. This includes:

Something to give up. The word to everyone after having heard the facts of the gospel is that there is something to give up, repent of, change your mind and direction from. You are going the wrong way and doing the wrong things to please God.

This is called repentance because of the "Fall" (a non-biblical word), which is used to describe what happened in the Garden of Eden and afterward. The original couple disobeyed the only command God gave them, and were expelled, and humankind has been hiding from God ever since. *"All we like sheep have gone astray; we have all turned to our own way, and the Lord has laid on him [Jesus] the iniquity of us all"* (Isaiah 53:6).

The New Testament terminology is: *"Since all have sinned and fall short of the glory of God"* (Romans 3:23). The imagery is of an archer shooting at a target. Despite how hard he pulls the string and aims the arrow, it always falls short. This is what happens when we try to please God out of our own efforts or in our own strength. This is why we need Jesus. *"Whoever has the Son has life; whoever does not have the Son of God does not have life"* (1 John 5:12). If we have Jesus, we have everything. If we don't have Jesus, we have nothing. With Jesus, we need nothing more, nothing less, and nothing else.

Something to believe. Paul tells us what needs to be believed as a bare minimum to be a Christian.

> Now I would remind you, brothers and sisters, of the good news that I proclaimed to you, which you in turn received, in which also you stand, through which also you are being saved… that Christ died for our sins in accordance with the [Old Testament] scriptures, and that he was buried, and that he was raised on the third day in accordance with the scriptures, and that he appeared to Cephas, then to the twelve. Then he appeared to more than five hundred brothers and sisters at one time, most of whom are still alive, though some have died. Then he appeared to James, then to all of the apostles. Last of all, as to one untimely born, he appeared also to me. (1 Corinthians 15:1-8)

This has been called *Mere Christianity* by C.S. Lewis, *Basic Christianity* by John Stott, and more recently *Simply Christian* by N.T. Wright. Or we could call it the Bare Bones Gospel. That's it! That's the bare minimum. You can believe more, and there is much more, but you cannot believe less and be a Christian! But someone might question, "Do I have to believe in the virgin birth? Is belief in the Trinity important? Do baptism and the Lord's Supper matter? Does church membership get me into heaven? Can't I just be a good person and hope for the best?" The answer is, if you could do any of these, Jesus would not have come. Belief in and receiving the Lord Jesus Christ is the first and only way to become a Christian. God makes this belief real by the work of his Holy Spirit in an internal change. As country singer George Jones sang about choosing:

> I've had choices since the day I was born,
> There've been voices that told me right
>   from wrong,
> If I had listened, I wouldn't be here today,
> Living and dying with the choices I've
>   made.[28]

Something to do. There are three simple steps to becoming a Christian: acknowledge our need, believe on the Lord Jesus Christ, and confess him before others. A few key Bible verses might help.

"But to all who received him, who believed in his name, he gave power to become children of God" (John 1:12).

"There is salvation in no one else, for there is no other name under heaven given among mortals by which we must be saved" (Acts 4:12).

"Because if you confess with your lips that Jesus is Lord and believe in your heart that God raised him from the dead, you will be saved" (Romans 10:9-10).

"Listen! I am standing at the door, knocking; if you hear my voice and open the door, I will come in to you and eat with you, and you with me" (Revelation 3:20).

Why should we choose Christ?

BECAUSE OF WHAT JESUS IS DOING NOW

Jesus is now in heaven. He has sent his Holy Spirit to be his invisible witness and convincer to bring us to faith. Jesus is praying for us and drawing and nudging us to himself. How? Consider the following example by Sheldon Van Auken. He wrote of the ten nudges, pushes, or pulls which God used to bring him back to faith:

1. A revision of the Book of Common Prayer.
2. A transition from a lapsed Anglican to a participant in order to fight the Prayer Book changes.
3. The death of a cousin.
4. Reading a biography of C.S. Lewis and studying at Oxford University in England
5. A line in a book ("the human soul was made to enjoy some object that is never fully given").
6. Seeing a vision of his wife's death and her reality to him.
7. Reading *The Lion, the Witch and the Wardrobe* by C.S. Lewis.
8. A letter from an author about his days at Oxford with C.S. Lewis
9. A new friend talking about Christianity.
10. Reading the first page of *Out of the Silent Planet* by C.S. Lewis, which said nothing about God.

His testimony was,

> At the bottom of the page, with as little fuss as the falling of an autumn leaf, I had returned to the Obedience—God was first in my life. His will was my will, I knew this suddenly and totally. I prayed. Christ, I thought, looked at me with forgiving eyes.[29]

As the hymn has it, "If I ask him to receive me, will he say me nay? Not till earth, and not till heaven pass away!"[30]

Have you chosen Christ? Would you like to?

Charlotte Elliott was a young, light-hearted woman who was not too serious about religion. Someone asked her if she was a Christian. She said at first, "Mind your own business!" but then said, "I'd like to be but don't know how."

The advice was, "Come just as you are." She did and at age forty-five, she wrote the hymn *Just As I Am*, which was used by the Billy Graham Evangelistic Association in all of its crusades as an invitation hymn.[31]

SEVENTEEN

What Is a Christian?
Part III

There is a third reference in the New Testament to what a Christian is.

> Yet if any of you suffers as a Christian, do not consider it a disgrace, but glorify God because you bear this name. (1 Peter 4:16)

This passage speaks about the challenge of being a Christian and tells us several things about what it means to follow and to serve Christ.

THE CHRISTIAN LIFE IS NOT EASY

This is the disciplined, discipleship part of the Christian life. It is the second half. Don't be surprised, Peter says, at the painful trial you are suffering (1 Peter 4:12) For the Jew, it was not a strange thing, or unusual, to be persecuted. It was normal and even expected. The Gentile, however, would wonder, "Why should I suffer for being Christian? I'm a nice person, a good person!" It would be a shock and surprise for some.

The plain fact is, not everyone will like you or love you if you declare for Christ, not even your own family members. You might find it an uphill battle trying to be faithful to Christ and serving Christ—on the job, in school, or with friends. We are not to please people, but to please Christ. Many have lost out because of this.

You will also have enemies you never thought of before: the world, the flesh, and the devil—the world out there and the world inside. Paul called it a struggle, even for a mature Christian (see Romans 7, and Ephesians 6:10-18). As has been said, "When you try to drown the old man, you find out he is a good swimmer!"

Hymn writer Isaac Watts asks:

> Must I be carried to the skies on flow'ry beds of ease, while others fought to win the prize and sailed thro' bloody seas? Are there no foes for me to face? Must I not stem the flood? Is this vile world a friend to grace, to help me on to God? Sure I must fight if I would win, increase my courage Lord; I'll bear the toil, endure the pain, supported by thy word.[32]

Think of the truth and wisdom behind these words, "It is easy to be a Christian where it is hard to be a Christian, and it is hard to be a Christian where it is easy to be a Christian."

THE CHRISTIAN LIFE IS PATTERNED AFTER CHRIST

Whatever happens to Christ happens to his followers. He was rejected and denied even by his own family for a time. As John wrote,

> He was in the world, and the world came into being through him; yet the world did not know him. He came to what was his own, but his own people did not accept him. (John 1:10-11)
> For not even his own brothers believed in him. (John 7:5)

If we truly follow Christ, his friends will be our friends, his enemies will be our enemies, his will will be our will, his life will be our life, and his end will be our end. Somewhere in the world right now, someone is suffering and giving their life for identifying with Christ. It could be in China, Indonesia, Africa, Russia, the Middle East, or even where you live.

You don't have to be martyred to suffer loss for Christ! Therefore accept it, rejoice in it, be glad, praise God for it, thank God for it, and receive his blessing and strength for it. It is a privilege!

At Urbana, on the University of Illinois Campus, Dr. Helen Rosevere gave her testimony of her missionary service in the Congo in the 1960s. During her torture and rape by the rebels, the Lord seemed to say to her, "These are not your sufferings, they are mine. I am just loaning your body." The experience was ultimately for her a privilege of sharing in the fellowship of the sufferings of Christ (Philippians 3:10).[33]

Joni Eareckson Tada became a quadriplegic at age sixteen. Instead of withdrawing in self-pity and anger, she went on to dedicate her life to helping and encouraging others with like disabilities.[34]

William Borden went to be a missionary in China, having renounced his business and family fortune in America. On the way, he died in Egypt of spinal meningitis in 1913, at the age of twenty-five. Afterwards, in his Bible were found the words written, "No Reserve, No Retreat, No Regrets."[35]

These examples are far from the soft success and self-centered "ouch-less" and "cross-less" Christianity of our day. Are we missing out on what the Christian life is all about?

THE CHRISTIAN LIFE IS A MODEL

No Christian should suffer as a murderer, or a thief, or any other kind of criminal, or even as a meddler, but should be a model and a mentor. There are the standards, morals, and ethics of the Christian life. This is what all of the New Testament books outside the Gospels tell us, how to behave and the consequences of not doing so.

The Christian should not be the same as any other with a little religion added. There should be and must be a difference. Paul said, *"Put to death, therefore, whatever in you is earthly... These are the ways you also once followed, when you were living that life. But now you must get rid of all such things"* (Colossians 3:5, 7-8).

Phillips Brooks, who wrote the Christmas carol "O Little Town of Bethlehem," was a failure as a teacher but had great success as a preacher. One day, the philosopher Josiah Royce was sitting in his study at Harvard University talking with a young student. The student asked the professor for a definition of a Christian. The philosopher replied, "I do not know how to define a Christian... But wait," he added, looking out the window, "there goes Phillips Brooks."[36]

The apostle Paul wrote his first letter to the Thessalonians and said they were a model church in every way—elect, exemplary, enthusiastic, and expectant. His basic message to them was, "We believe that Jesus died and rose again. God will bring back Jesus. Jesus will not come alone. There will still be believers when he does come. The dead in Christ will be raised first, and the living will be changed. His coming is personal, physical, and powerful. There is encouragement and comfort in these truths. There should be a difference" (paraphrased from 1 Thessalonians 1:4-10, 4:13-18)

Jesus is our model. Hollywood is not our model. The business world is not our model. The sports world is not our model. The science/academic world is not our model. As a Christian professor once said in a lecture to first-year students about the total university and academic experience, "The answer is there is no answer." As a Christian, he later qualified his answer, "The answer is, Christ is the answer."

THE CHRISTIAN LIFE HAS AN END IN SIGHT

We are not aimlessly stumbling along waiting for our end to come. There is a purpose, a will, an end, and a goal to following Christ as a Christian. What is that? There is a judgment of accountability coming to all. God seems to be harder on his own, as Peter reminds us,

> For the time has come for judgment to begin with the household of God; if it begins with us, what will be the end for those who do not obey the gospel of God? And "If it is hard for the righteous to be saved, what will become of the ungodly and the sinners?" (1 Peter 4:17-18)

Clearly, there are some who won't pass the test and will be sorry!

There is a narrow way and Jesus is the only door. There is a cost for following Jesus. Think about it and see if you are ready. Jesus said in each of the gospels that there is a price for following him. What should we do?

COMMIT TO A FAITHFUL CREATOR

God is our keeper, protector, sustainer, strength, purpose, and end. We can trust him! Think of the example of Alexander Cruden. He wrote Cruden's Concordance of the Bible in the seventeenth century, which is still used today as a standard reference to the Bible. He suffered greatly for his faith.

He was illegally confined to a madhouse three times for extended periods. While there, he recited the psalms and committed all of them to memory. He said of his determination to do the will of God,

> If I had a hundred hairs to hang by, and
> ninety-nine should fail, I would endeavour
> to hang by the hundredth, and if that
> should fail I then submit to the will of
> God.[37]

We must have better Christians. The church must find its voice again and backbone and its ability to say "NO" and lead to a positive "YES." Jim Eliot was a missionary to Ecuador and was martyred along with others. Before going, he said, "He is no fool who gives up what he cannot keep to gain that which he cannot lose."[38] Was his life for nothing?

CONTINUE TO DO GOOD

We are left here to do good, not to sit on our hands, twiddle our thumbs, and satisfy ourselves. Jesus said, "You are the salt of the earth," not the sugar. "You are the light of the world," not the life of the party (see Matthew 5:13-16). We are to preserve, give flavour, bite and cut into, and challenge societal norms and failures. We are not to sweeten and sugarcoat the gospel and its demands and challenges.

We are to attract, give light and wisdom and understanding and discernment to what is going on. We are to point out the sins and wrongs and point to the solution in our Lord

Jesus Christ. Here is the challenge of being a Christian and suffering for Christ.

So we must ask ourselves, am I a Christian then?

Has there been a change?

Have I made a choice for Christ?

Have I taken up the challenge?

EIGHTEEN

The Promises
of Leadership

There are about fifteen promises of "I will" or "I shall" in Psalm 101. They are the promises of leadership. Historically, it is the commitment and covenant of a king for his son at a time of coronation or installation, either of David or Solomon. This psalm is a resolve to do better than before. It is a commitment to clean house. It is a pattern for anyone in a position leadership to change.

Life is filled with promises of "I will." Consider the following:

A man and woman exchange their wedding vows, saying, "I promise to have and to hold, from this day forward, in sickness and in health, for richer or poorer, to love and to cherish as long as we both shall live." They exchange rings and say they will keep their promise to each other.

Parents are asked at the presentation of their children in dedication, "Do you promise to raise this child in the Christian way?" They say, "I will." Children in return are expected to love, honour, and obey.

Employers and employees agree to an unwritten contract of job performance which means, "I will, I do, I promise to do a fair day's work for a fair day's pay."

Citizens and the society they live in make a common contract of promise to be good, law-abiding citizens.

Christians are asked to make a commitment to Jesus Christ with such words as, "Do you take Jesus Christ as your Lord and Saviour? Will you trust him, serve him, honour him, worship him, and obey him?" The expected response is, "I promise, I will."

Church members or adherents are asked, "Do you, will you support, serve, give, commit, and become a part of this church and fellowship?" The answer is, "I do, I will."

Let us consider this psalm in its various categories of truth to test our loyalty and commitment, as the king did. What kind of life does this show us?

A WORSHIPPING LIFE

"I will sing of loyalty and of justice; to you, O Lord, I will sing" (Psalm 101:1).

This supposes a certain level of commitment and allegiance to God as Lord and Saviour, or to Jesus Christ for the Christian. This person, at whatever age, has bowed the head and the knee to acknowledge Lordship to someone higher, better, sovereign—God. This means that the boss has a boss who is worthy of loyalty, love, and praise. This is first. You can't be a Christian without it.

A WORTHY LIFE

"I will study the way that is blameless. When shall I attain it?" (Psalm 101:2)

This is a very high ideal, which neither David nor Solomon attained in their reign, before or after they became king. But does this mean that it should not be striven for or sought after? Jesus said, *"Be perfect, therefore, as your heavenly Father is perfect"* (Matthew 5:48). Paul said, *"Be imitators of me"* (1 Corinthians 4:16), and *"Be imitators of me, as I am of Christ"* (1 Corinthians 11:1).

It is a standard, a benchmark, a goal, and a model for attainment. "Ah, but a man's reach should exceed his grasp, or what's a heaven for?"[39] We struggle and strive, work and pray, trust and believe, fail and get up and move ahead. This is life.

"I urge you to live a life worthy of the calling you have received. Be completely humble and gentle; be patient, bearing with one another in love" (Ephesians 4:1-2, NIV).

"And we pray this in order that you may live a life worthy of the Lord and may please him in every way" (Colossians 1:10, NIV).

This is the standard to which we strive—a worthy life, which includes fears, failure, frustration, and false hopes, but also faith, fulfillment, joy, satisfaction, and arrival.

AN OPEN LIFE

"I will walk with integrity of heart within my house" (Psalm 101:2).

David did not do very well in his house. His sins included adultery, murder, and cover-up, as well as condoning incest and revenge killing among his children. He also had a weak will in disciplining his boys and brought shame on the nation (see 2 Samuel 11-12).

Many have difficulty with an open life, exposed to the world or to God. Does God care what goes on in my house? The answer is yes!

A prime minister of Canada once said, "The state has no business in the bedrooms of the nation."[40] If the government has no business in our private lives, does God? God sees in secret and will bring it out into the open. We don't tell all to all, but we are open to God, and seek to walk with integrity of heart. This is a problem in almost every walk of life— openness, integrity, and honesty. Think of the examples of Enron, WorldCom, presidents, and others in places of trust and authority who have failed. But the promise must be made—I promise, I will.

A DISCIPLINED LIFE

"I will not set before my eyes anything that is base" (Psalm 101:3)

This is likewise a difficult task. The eye-gate is the entranceway to many and varied temptations. Jesus said: *"If your right eye causes you to sin, tear it out and throw it away; it is better for you to lose one of your members than for your whole body to be thrown into hell. And if your right hand causes you to sin, cut it off and throw it away"* (Matthew 5:29-30). This severity of action is meant figuratively, not literally. It means a disciplined life. It means being able to say yes or no, or don't go there, or don't look, buy, possess, or handle something, and to have the courage and strength from God to do it.

As Job said, *"I have made a covenant with my eyes; how then could I look upon a virgin?"* (Job 31:1). And as Paul admonished, *"Let the same mind be in you that was in Christ Jesus"* (Philippians 2:5), and *"Finally, beloved, whatever is true, whatever is honorable, whatever is just, whatever is pure, whatever is pleasing, whatever is commendable, if there is any excellence and if there is anything worthy of praise, think about these things"* (Philippians 4:8).

About testing he said, *"No testing has overtaken you that is not common to everyone. God is faithful, and he will not let you be tested beyond your strength, but with the testing he will also provide the way out so that you may be able to endure it"* (1 Corinthians 10:13). Personally, God told Paul that the thorn in his flesh would not be taken away, but that, *"My grace is sufficient for you, for power is made perfect in weakness"* (2 Corinthians 12:9).

The Christian life is not an easy life, but it can be a blessed and victorious as we submit to God's discipline.

AN EXCLUSIVE LIFE

"I will not set before my eyes anything that is base. I hate the work of those who fall away; it shall not cling to me. Perverseness of heart shall be far from me; I will know nothing of evil. One who secretly slanders a neighbour I will destroy. A haughty look and an arrogant heart I will not tolerate... No one who practices deceit shall remain in my house; no one who utters lies shall continue in my presence" (Psalm 101:3-5,7).

The next few verses show that, as a leader, there are certain things and types of people that must be excluded from one's life: those who fall away, the one who secretly slanders a neighbour, the one with the haughty look and arrogant heart, the one who practices deceit, and the one who utters lies.

This is why Paul said in the New Testament,

> Do not be mismatched with unbelievers... what does a believer share with an unbeliever?... Therefore come out from them, and be separate from them, says the Lord, and touch nothing unclean; then I will welcome you. (2 Corinthians 6:14-15, 17)

Being a Christian leader and model, to be used of God, must involve exclusion, being apart, and achieving separation from unbecoming behaviour. In a sense, you can't run with the crowd and lead the crowd at the same time. As an example of this, Prince Ernest the Pious in the seventeenth century sent an unfaithful minister a copy of Psalm 101 to read and to heed, which became a proverb for others.[41] To exclude might not make a leader popular, or make friends, or get attention or promotions, but they get to keep their soul! This exclusion might even include some very innocent and simple things in life to which God may say, "Stay away from it or give it up."

AN INCLUSIVE LIFE

"I will look with favor on the faithful in the land, so that they may live with me; whoever walks in the way that is blameless shall minister to me" (Psalm 101:6).

This tells us who should be included in our circle of friends and confidants. This takes discernment, maturity, faith, patience, and trust. Who do you trust? Who gives you advice? Think of the kings of Israel. Who were their friends and confidants, and where did it take them?

Think of David and his rise to power, or Solomon and his fall, Rehoboam and the splitting up of the kingdom, and Hezekiah and Josiah, who brought reformation and revival to the nation. We might need to ask ourselves, who will be in my administration? Who will be my public face, speak for me, and act on my behalf? Who are my intimates, my confidants? You can tell where you are going and what kind of success or failure you will have by your inclusive life.

A WISE LIFE

The king speaks of his daily habit and routine of dispensing justice and equity in the land. He had a job to do and was at it: *"Morning by morning I will destroy all the wicked in the land, cutting off all evildoers from the city of the Lord"* (Psalm 101:8).

One need not be a king to administer judgment, discernment, and discrimination in the office to which one has been chosen, appointed, or elected. In the New Testament and modern context, the wisdom is to be able to do this with equity, fairness, and consistency. This is a difficult task, but leaders must do it as part of their mandate. It is easy to compromise, give in, cheat, lower the standard, and accept second best, but is it good, godly, or wise?

Archbishop Donald Coggin relates that each ordained Bishop or Archbishop of the Church of England receives a copy of the Holy Scriptures with the challenge to be faithful in proclaiming them in their ministries.[42]

At the ordination of every minister, pastor, priest, elder, or deacon in most denominations, the question is asked, "Do you, will you?" regarding matters of commitment and dedication. We suggest that the Lord Jesus will ask on the Day of Judgment, "Have you? Did you? Why not?"

In light of the above, there may be questions we need to ask ourselves: Are there promises we have made and not kept? Are there commitments and areas to which we need to say, "I will, I promise"? Is this a time to get things right and make our promises to the Lord?

NINETEEN

The Right Spirit in Leadership

Having the right spirit or attitude in leadership is vitally important, especially for the spiritual leader. How we approach God and the attitude we have toward him is a key to our worship and spiritual well-being.

Psalm 51, as penned by King David, is about one's spiritual attitude toward God. It is considered David's prayer of confession and repentance when Nathan the prophet confronted him about his sin with Bathsheba and his cover-up of it by having her husband Uriah killed in battle (see 2 Samuel 11-12).

Four times, the word "spirit" is mentioned in this psalm: *"a new and right spirit"* (51:10), the *"holy spirit"* (51:11), *"a willing spirit"* (51:12), and *"a broken spirit"* (51:17). Two others are implied: the right spirit (prior to the writing), and the wrong spirit (51:1-5), after his sin and fall.

RIGHT SPIRIT

We begin with this because this is a prayer and song of a believer, not an unbeliever. From the New Testament perspective, David was a Christian. At some point in his youth, perhaps from a godly line, David came to know the Lord. When Boaz married faithful Ruth, a son was born.

"They named him Obed; he became the father of Jesse, the father of David" (Ruth 4:17). Out on the windswept hills around Bethlehem and on the cold dark nights while watching sheep, David found a close friend. It took the shiver out of his bones and the fear out of his heart. He believed, *"The Lord is my shepherd, I shall not want"* (Psalm 23:1).

As a young man, he was brought in before Samuel, *"Then Samuel took the horn of oil, and anointed him in the presence of his brothers; and the spirit of the Lord came mightily upon David from that day forward"* (1 Samuel 16:13).

David became a mature believer. He defeated Goliath and all of Israel's enemies. He survived Saul's attempts to kill him and finally became king of Judah and Israel.

He could say with the apostle Paul, *"I know the one in whom I have put my trust, and I am sure that he is able to guard until that day what I have entrusted to him"* (2 Timothy 1:12).

WRONG SPIRIT

Something went wrong with David's spirit and in his relationship with God. What was it?

We might suggest it was "spring urges."

"In the spring of the year, the time when kings go out to battle, David sent Joab with his officers… But David remained at Jerusalem. It happened, late one afternoon… that he saw from the roof a woman bathing; the woman was very beautiful" (2 Samuel 11:1-2). And the rest is history! It could also be a mid-life crisis; he saw, desired, took, and tried to cover it up. David's wrong spirit is shown in his double standard.

He became a hypocrite, governing and judging for one whole year before being brought to account by God. Added to this was a hard heart and resistance to change. David had to hear the words of self-condemnation, *"You are the man!"* (2 Samuel 12:7). We should thank God for anyone sent from God who tells us that we have a wrong spirit.

BROKEN SPIRIT

David said, "The sacrifice acceptable to God is a broken spirit; a broken and contrite heart, O God, you will not despise." (Psalm 51:17) This was the spirit David expressed in his multi-petition prayer to God:

> Have mercy on me… blot out my transgressions. Wash me from my iniquity, and cleanse me from my sin. For I know my transgressions, and my sin is ever before

me. Against you, you alone, have I sinned,
and done what is evil in your sight, so that
you are justified in your sentence and
blameless when you pass judgment. Indeed,
I was born guilty, a sinner when my mother
conceived me. (Psalm 51:1-5)

As Lancelot Andrewes summarized his own life,

Two things I recognize, O Lord, in myself;
Nature, which thou hast made;
Sin, which I have added…
Lord, as we add day to day;
So sin to sin.[43]

David's prayer was like the thief on the cross who said,
*"we are getting what we deserve for our deeds, but this man has
done nothing wrong… Jesus, remember me when you come into
your kingdom"* (Luke 23:41- 42). It was like the prodigal son
who confessed, *"Father, I have sinned against heaven and before you; I am no longer worthy to be called your son"* (Luke
15:18-19). It was like Peter's exclamation, *"Go away from me,
Lord, for I am a sinful man!"* (Luke 5:8) It was like Paul's personal testimony, *"The saying is sure and worthy of full acceptance, that Christ Jesus came into the world to save sinners—of
whom I am the foremost"* (1 Timothy 1:15).

Without reference to an extended argument on original
sin, this is the spirit that delights God and is acceptable to
him. It is the one he saves and heals.

RENEWED SPIRIT

David is asking God in this psalm to do something new for him. *"Create in me a clean heart, O God, and put a new and right spirit within me"* (Psalm 51:10). Note his openness and positive attitude toward God once he is broken before him.

> You desire truth in the inward being; there-
> fore teach me wisdom in my secret heart.
> Purge me with hyssop, and I shall be clean;
> wash me, and I shall be whiter than snow.
> Let me hear joy and gladness; let the bones
> that you have crushed rejoice. Hide your
> face from my sins, and blot out all my iniq-
> uities. (Psalm 51:6-9)

David could never have said these words before he was broken. Now he wants God to do his full work, holding back and hiding nothing.

HOLY SPIRIT

"Do not cast me away from your presence, and do not take your holy spirit from me" (Psalm 51:11). Although there is not a developed theology or teaching about the person of the Holy Spirit until we get to the man of the Spirit, Jesus Christ in the New Testament, there can be no doubt that the Spirit came on many Old Testament people for special tasks and duties. This was David's experience as noted above (1 Samuel 16:13).

David's prayer gives the hint that he is concerned about losing his salvation and the assurance of God's presence with him. Is this possible? He may have in mind Saul's experience: *"Now the spirit of the Lord departed from Saul, and an evil spirit from the Lord tormented him"* (1 Samuel 16:14), and *"Saul was afraid of David, because the Lord was with him but had departed from Saul"* (1 Samuel 18:12).

Paul talked about disciplining or punishing his body so that when he preached to others he would not be disqualified, or become *"a castaway"* (1 Corinthians 9:27, KJV). He also talked about grieving the Holy Spirit (Ephesians 4:30), and the possibility that one could *"quench the Spirit"* (1 Thessalonians 5:19).

The writer to the Hebrews tells us that it is impossible to restore someone who has fallen away, even if they *"have shared in the Holy Spirit"* (6:4).

He further describes some who might have *"outraged the Spirit of grace"* (10:29). But no examples are given of those who have actually been cut off for this!

We should note that this is a subject which may require further study and time, especially in a discussion group, but the key for David and anyone concerned about their condition before God is to pray, *"Restore to me the joy of your salvation"* (Psalm 51:12). It is the Holy Spirit who lists the fruit of the Spirit as *"love, joy, peace, patience, kindness, generosity, faithfulness, gentleness, and self-control"* (Galatians 5:22-23). Notice that fruit is collective like a bunch of grapes, not singular as one fruit at a time. All is given by the Holy Spirit and develops as a whole.

WILLING SPIRIT

David prayed, *"Sustain in me a willing [or free or generous] spirit"* (Psalm 51:12). This is the key that sustains volunteerism and missions in the service of God. It is the reason why so many in Christian service find themselves stressed out and exhausted. It is the want of a willing spirit on the part of those who will not serve. People drag their feet, resist, oppose, and even become antagonistic toward God. When there is a willing spirit, the oil flows and the way becomes easy and clear. This comes from God. Think of these New Testament examples:

When the seven deacons in the early church were to be chosen, the instruction was to *"select from among yourselves seven men of good standing, full of the Spirit and of wisdom, whom we may appoint to this task"* (Acts 6:3). This includes a willing spirit.

When the church was to include the Gentiles, the word went out on what restrictions should be required. The directive was, "it has seemed good to the Holy Spirit and to us…" (Acts 15:28). There was agreement, unity, willingness, and a free and generous spirit.

When Paul was collecting an offering for the poor saints in Jerusalem, he wrote to the Corinthian church about the example and generosity of the Macedonians, who, during a severe ordeal of affliction, their abundant joy and their extreme poverty have overflowed in a wealth of generosity on their part... they voluntarily gave according to their means, and even beyond their means, begging us earnestly for the privilege of sharing in this ministry to the saints—and this, not merely as we expected; they gave themselves first to the Lord and, by the will of God, to us. (2 Corinthians 8:2-5)

This is the willing spirit David prays for, and the very thing that is often lacking in the church today. And by praying this, it opened him up and freed him to possibilities never before available. And the results were: *"Then I will teach transgressors your ways, and sinners will return to you... my tongue will sing aloud of your deliverance. O Lord, open my lips, and my mouth will declare your praise"* (Psalms 51:13-15). Do you want God to use you? Ask for a "willing spirit." You won't be disappointed.

TWENTY

Weather Watch

Many are concerned about global warming and the unusual change in weather patterns that many countries are experiencing. Should the Christian be concerned about this aside from an ecological responsibility and the conservation of natural resources entrusted to us by a benevolent and gracious Creator?

Jesus was challenged by the sceptical religious leaders of his day to show them a sign from heaven. He answered,

> "When it is evening, you say, 'It will be fair weather, for the sky is red.' And in the morning, 'It will be stormy today, for the sky is red and threatening.' You know how to interpret the appearance of the sky, but you cannot interpret the signs of the times. An evil and adulterous generation asks for a sign, but no sign will be given to it except

the sign of Jonah." Then he left them and
went away. (Matthew 16:2-4)

Jesus is telling us that it is not a weather watch that
should concern us, but a resurrection watch. Jesus died, was
buried, and was raised on the third day, like the experience of
the prophet Jonah being in the fish's belly for three days and
nights and then being spewed out. It is the challenge and
change that comes from that cataclysmic event that should
shape and focus our attention.

If resurrection does not move us in the right direction
and motivate us to look somewhere else besides our own
bellybutton, civilization and even the church is in serious
trouble.

In the early days of the church, the good news of the resurrection of Jesus turned the world upside down, or right side
up, depending on our view of reality. Today, it appears not to
be making the same impact, except in the reports of massive
conversions in China and Africa where the gospel has had a
hard time being rooted in the twenty-first century. As it has
been said elsewhere, "It is hard to be a Christian where it is
easy to be a Christian, and it is easy to be a Christian where it
is hard to be a Christian."

But what of the weather watch? Jesus later quoted the
prophet Joel in saying that the really big changes, like *"the sun
will be darkened, and the moon will not give its light; the stars
will fall from heaven, and the powers of heaven will be shaken"*
(Matthew 24:29), will result in the second coming of Christ

and the upheaval of judgment and the end of the world (see Joel 2:30-32 and Acts 2:17-21). This is not then.

Until then, the believer is to watch, wait, work, and worship until the call comes. Things around us, including the weather, may fluctuate, change, and even become scary and threatening. The Christian is to be patient, believing, trusting, and committed to sharing the good news of Jesus and the resurrection whenever and wherever possible.

TWENTY-ONE
Leadership Two

Aleader or pastor is someone who shows certain qualities or characteristics of leadership, which are pictured in Psalm 106. The primary characters are Moses and Phinehas, who both stood up and interceded or stood in the gap during the seven failures or sins of ancient Israel. But there were seven basic leadership qualities, which each revealed. The modern spiritual servant of the Lord should show the same thing.

SELECTED

Anyone who acts as a mediator in leadership is in some way selected. Moses was God's chosen one, and Phinehas was the grandson of Aaron, Moses' brother, and a priest by succession. Both were selected, like all of the Old Testament patriarchs, prophets, judges, kings, and leaders. This is likewise true of the disciples of Jesus and the early leaders of the Christian church. It was the same experience of the women who served in both the Old and New Testament eras. As Jesus said, *"You did not choose me but I chose you"* (John 15:16), and *"As the Father has sent me, so I send you"* (John 20:21). God is still selecting and sending servants.

SENSED

Those who have been selected and chosen have sensed it. There has been a stirring, a moving of the heart, a feeling of being set apart, or being different.

A study of personality traits of forty-one American presidents found that they were dominators, introverted, good guys, the innocents, actors, the maintainers, philosophers, or intellectuals and extroverts. Some fit into more than one category.[44]

Psychiatrist M. Scott Peck quotes Professor Arnold Ludwig's study titled *The Price of Greatness*, which examines the lives of 1,004 eminent figures of the twentieth century, including artists, writers, inventors, and others. They all showed the following characteristics: a readiness to disregard prevalent views, an irreverence toward established authority, a strong capacity for solitude, and a "psychological unease."[45]

As an example of this sensing that one is special or superior, Peck tells the case of treating a young woman whose experience on dates, with other students, professors, and friends was that everyone she encountered were pompous, limited, unimaginative, dull, and not very bright. Peck asked her to consider that she might in fact be superior to them and should accept her superiority. Her query was that everyone is equal with the response, "Are they?" The problem is how to accept the "elite or superior sense" without becoming a snob, proud, self-righteous, or arrogant. It is how to challenge the status quo, the culture, the accepted standards, and to rise above the times or influence them or change them. Is this a curse or a calling?[46]

Many go through this questioning of their sense of calling as Moses, Joseph, Paul, and Jesus did.

As the Abbe de Tourville advised his young inquirer:

> There is nothing presumptuous in believing and feeling that one is right. In fact it is absolutely essential to become accustomed to such spiritual confidence. If we don't do this we fail to see things clearly and so get in a great muddle.[47]

SUFFERED

Those who have been selected by God and have sensed it have suffered for it. They are made to pay their dues and show scars and wounds for their visions and dreams of grandeur. Take the following biblical characters as examples:

Joseph's dreams cost him thirteen years in either obscurity or prison. Moses assumed that God's people would understand that God had selected him as their deliverer, *"but they did not"* (Acts 7:25). This was painful and cost him forty years in the wilderness. Job suffered months of painful losses and almost perished from the false accusations of his friends.

John the Baptist had to live apart from society for most of his life in order that he might challenge that same society to live for God and accept their Messiah. Jesus spent eighteen years in obscurity before he was ready to do his work of redemption. Paul lost at least ten years sitting on the shelf because his dramatic conversion was too hot to handle by those whom he had previously persecuted.

The Wizard of Id comic strip illustrated this with the picture of the king just being missed by an arrow, which sticks in a tree with a note attached. "It's from the mob," said his attendant. The note says, "Could you move just a tad to the left?" Anyone seeking to lead or to mediate a conflict will suffer and become a target.

SERVED

Leaders who are called to "come up higher" are ones who are already serving. They do not say, "I should be so and so," or "I should be in such and such position or place." They grow where they are planted. There may not be much room at the top, but there is plenty of room at the bottom, so start there!

God is the one who will lift up and exalt you in his own time. Think of the case of Joseph, who ran errands for his father with a coloured coat on. Ruth was only looking for food and security for her mother-in-law when she was sent to glean in Boaz's fields. She ended up in the messianic line. Amos was a simple farmer who was called to be a prophet to

God's people. Daniel was a young captive in Babylon who by his wisdom rose to be chief council to kings. Two pairs of fisherman brothers were chosen by Jesus to be his followers. Three were in his inner circle. As Peter later assures us, *"Humble yourselves therefore under the mighty hand of God, so that he may exalt you in due time"* (1 Peter 5:6).

SENT

Being sent may come before serving in order, but it is important in leadership. Those who have been selected, have sensed it, have suffered for it, and are serving have a timing element to their work in being sent at just the right time. Think of these biblical examples.

Moses was raised up when the four hundred years of Israel's time in Egypt were completed and they began to cry to God for deliverance. God had him ready.

Phinehas stopped a plague just at the right time when twenty-four thousand people were killed.

When the captive Jewish nation was threatened with genocide under the Persian Empire, Esther, who had providentially become queen, was assured by her uncle, *"Who knows? Perhaps you have come to royal dignity for such a time as this"* (Esther 4:14).

Jesus came into the world not at any time, *"but when the fullness of time had come, God sent his Son"* (Galatians 4:4), to redeem us all.

Historically, great military leaders such as Churchill, Patton, and MacArthur had the same sense of timing for their leadership in time of war. When timing is everything, God's servants are sent.

SACRIFICED

Some leaders have been sacrificed for the cause they were sent to meet and resolve. Our text tells us that God's people *"angered the Lord at the waters of Meribah, and it went ill with Moses on their account; for they made his spirit bitter, and he spoke words that were rash"* (Psalm 106:32-33). This kept Moses out of the Promised Land. It is possible for pastors and leaders to lose out because of the stubbornness and disobedience of the very people they are called to lead and serve. Some get caught up in the sins of the people, become discouraged, and break down, pack up and quit the ministry. Sometimes they are expendable and are sacrificial lambs for the cause of Christ, as Paul reminds us: *"For your sake we are being killed all day long; we are accounted as sheep to be slaughtered"* (Romans 8:36).

SATISFIED

Those who take up the calling and serve are in the end satisfied and complete, without regret. As the psalmist prays,

> Remember me, O Lord, when you show favor to your people; help me when you deliver them; that I may see the prosperity of your chosen ones, that I may rejoice in the

gladness of your nation, that I may glory in
your heritage. (Psalm 106:4-5)

As Goethe, the eighteenth century German poet, reminds us,

> Every extraordinary man has a certain mis-
> sion to accomplish. If he has fulfilled it, he
> is no longer needed on earth in the same
> form, and Providence uses him for some-
> thing else. Mozart died at age 36 years, so
> did Raphael, and Lord Byron a little
> older... But all these had perfectly fulfilled
> their mission; and it was time for them to
> depart, that other people might still have
> something to do in a world made to last a
> long time.[48]

This means that those who have been selected as leaders
have sensed it, suffered for it, served, been sent and sacrificed,
and have been satisfied in their work, and God has been satisfied with them. Because of Phinehas' heroic stand against sin,
the plague was stopped, *"And that has been reckoned to him as
righteousness from generation to generation forever"* (Psalm
106:31). You can't get better satisfaction than that!

And to summarize Moses' great work, the writer said,

> Never since has there arisen a prophet in Is-
> rael like Moses, whom the Lord knew face
> to face. He was unequaled for all the signs
> and wonders... and for all the mighty deeds

and all the terrifying displays of power that
Moses performed in the sight of all Israel.
(Deuteronomy 34:10-12)

He was the benchmark, the standard, the model, the example, and the book was closed.

SAMPLE

Paul referred to these times and incidents as samples and
examples that God has given to keep us from the same sins,
follies, failings, and consequences as the ancients. They were
written down for us to learn not to be arrogant, proud, stubborn, or disobedient. But God is faithful. He will keep us,
watch over us, hold back temptation from us, bear us up, and
provide a way to escape if need be (see 1 Corinthians 10:6-
13). He has given Jesus Christ our Lord to be our mediator,
Saviour, and strong deliverer we can believe, trust, obey, follow, and so be able to say with the Psalmist, *"Blessed be to the
Lord, the God of Israel, from everlasting to everlasting. And let
all the people say, 'Amen.' Praise the Lord!"* (Psalm 106:48).

TWENTY-TWO
The Play of God

D o you love to play? Do you love poetry and music and the arts? God does! He shows us in Psalm 114 and 117 that he is the God of play.

In the context of Psalm 114, there are several images used to describe what the psalmist sees—a spiritual image where Judah is God's sanctuary and Israel is his dominion; a liberating image where God's people are released from four hundred years of captivity; a geographical image where the Red Sea and the Jordan river flee and are turned back; an ecological image about mountains and hills, and pools and springs of water; an animal image of rams and lambs; and a universal image in Psalm 117 of everything and everyone and everything praising God. It is the language of the poet, the mystic, the artist, and the visionary where in simile and metaphor the sea has eyes and runs away, the river is stopped by stepping into it, the mountains skip and jump and tremble, and the hard rocks become pools and springs of joy and gladness. This is nature at play and we are invited to jump in and enjoy it.

It tells us that when normal language becomes too much for us to understand God and his wonderful acts and deeds, then the words of the prophet, poet, mystic, artist and visionary take over. These are the ones who see through and beyond and under something to its true meaning, depth, and spiritual importance

Think of the following examples.

When the apostle John was in exile and in the Spirit on the Lord's Day, he wrote the book of Revelation. In it he saw visions and images, types and likenesses to what he saw and knew on earth. He saw one like the Son of man. He saw angels, churches, elders, a Lamb, stars, a scroll, seals, horses, trumpets, plagues, a woman and dragon at war, beasts, judgment, a river, and a new heaven and earth. And we are still trying to translate that vision and to understand the images and what they mean for us today.

When the apostle Paul was finishing his majestic exposition of Romans and the mysteries of God, in a sense he threw up his hands and exclaimed, *"O the depth of the riches and wisdom and knowledge of God! How unsearchable are his judgments and how inscrutable his ways!"* (Romans 11:33). We can add to this list the works and words of such biblical writers as Moses, Ezekiel, Isaiah, Jeremiah, Job, the Psalmists, and Solomon in the Song of Songs as they sought to describe what they did not understand.

Poet Emily Dickinson said, "A word is dead when it is said, some say; I say it just begins to live that day." [49] How do we see and understand things?

As Malcolm Muggeridge quoted poet William Blake, "We must not only see with the eye, but through the eye." [50] Blake looked at a grain of sand and saw eternity in it. How could he? Consider the following case. Samuel Taylor Coleridge, at age nineteen, on November 13, 1797, went for a walk with the poet Wordsworth and his wife Dorothy. At 4:00 p.m., at the sunset looking out to sea, he saw an allegory of a man shooting an albatross (seagull) and wrote "The Rime of the Ancient Mariner." [51] Who gave him that thought?

George Frederick Handel was reading a verse in Job, *"I know that my redeemer liveth"* (Job 19:25), and wrote his famous oratorio The Messiah. [52]

Think how Jesus looked at a mustard seed and saw a kingdom, how he heard about a man being beaten and told the story of the Good Samaritan, and how he saw sheep straying and told of the lost sheep, the lost coin, and the lost son. Some forty times he told stories from common and everyday things of life.

Annie Dillard tells us what astronomers have discovered through the Hubble telescope:

> 80 billion galaxies, nine for each of us; each galaxy has 100 billion suns. Our galaxy the Milky Way has 400 billion suns, 69 for each one of us; the astronomers have been nickel and diming us to death—Does anyone be-

lieve the galaxies exist to add splendour to
the night sky over Bethlehem?[53]

Andrew Lloyd Weber saw something in the stories of *Jesus Christ Superstar*, *Cats*, *Les Miserables*, *The Phantom of the Opera*, and *Joseph and the Amazing Technicolor Dreamcoat* and wrote musicals to the delight of millions.

Canadian writer Pierre Burton was seeking inspiration to write about the Klondike gold rush and reached back to read the Christian allegory *Pilgrim's Progress*, written by a seventeenth century imprisoned pastor.[54] And think of what kind of world Walt Disney saw in a mouse and what became of it!

What do all of these things confirm to us? They tell us a lot! They tell us God uses many things to confirm his Word to us. We are not alone as we pass through this world. This world is full of play, poetry, music, art, and special effects and it comes from the God of play. The Bible and nature are full of this kind of life and rejoice in it.

We are to use God's gifts to help us through to the other side, where there is eternal play in the presence of God. Think what play does for the terminally ill, the depressed, or those challenged in any way because of some limitation of their humanity. God uses music, drama, art, and poetry. He also uses pets, and many other forms, to reach us and minister to us. So away with dull faces and long chins; rejoice and be glad. Think of the implications.

When we are under stress and uncertain about the future, a glance at the victories and assurances of the past can give great encouragement and strength for the future. If Jesus sang these psalms before going to the cross, think what help they can be to us. If nature jumps up and down over deliverance, exodus, victory, miraculous supply, and invention, what will resurrection bring? If Jesus said there is a party in heaven when a sinner repents and angels are doing cartwheels (Luke 15:1-10), what happens when we are right with God? If the sea and rivers are falling over one another to praise God, if mountains and hills are so animated that they jump and skip like new born lambs and rams, we could use a little kicking up of our heels! We, too, can be exuberant and playful with celebration and joy. This is the play of God.

A young six-year-old asks her friend, "Can you come out and play?" Jesus invites us to do the same when he asked, *"Who is greatest in the kingdom of heaven?"* (Matthew 18:1), and then he put a child in the midst and said, "Become like this child, change and become humble, welcome this child, don't put a stumbling block before her, or you'll be sorry" (paraphrased).

Isaiah said the future kingdom will have groupings of a wolf and lamb, a leopard and kid, a calf and lion together, and a little child leading them (Isaiah 11:6-9). What if along with praise and worship, "play" is the main occupation of heaven? Shouldn't we start here?

TWENTY-THREE
In the Gap Praying

Some believe that the church has lost its prayer power and is weak and anaemic when it comes to resisting the enemy and winning the spiritual battles of the day. R. Arthur Matthews said, "The church has lost her attack power."[55] Has she?

But Abraham stood in the gap for Israel and did intercede for Sodom and Gomorrah to rescue his nephew Lot. Moses did the same several times when Israel sinned in the wilderness and God threatened to do away with them. Paul likewise said that his burden and concern for Israel according to the flesh was so intense that he could wish himself accursed or cut off by God in order to have them saved (Romans 9:3). And Jesus did the same for our sins when he prayed in the Garden of Gethsemane for deliverance from the cross. Luke says his sweat was like drops of blood and that an angel had to come and strengthen him for the task ahead (Luke 22:43-44).

Those who have been great prayers have had certain characteristics that have set them apart as those who received great things from God. They have been specific about their prayers. They seemed to know what the outcome would be. They were burdened and focused on their goal. They were persistent and did not give up. Consider the following.

Ezekiel says there was a time when God *"sought for anyone among them who would repair the wall and stand in the breach before me on behalf of the land, so that I would not destroy it; but I found no one"* (Ezekiel 22:30). So he sent destruction.

A term used of those who prevailed in prayer with God in the past was a "prayer warrior." Jeremiah suggested that Moses and Samuel were that kind of person (Jeremiah 15:1 and Psalm 99:6). Ezekiel said that Noah, Daniel, and Job were the kind of righteous men who could hold back the judgment of God (Ezekiel 14:14, 20). Is it time for the church to gain back her attack power again, so she can stand in the gap for the land to preserve it from judgment?

D.M. McIntrye said of a great prayer warrior, "The devil is aware that one hour of close fellowship, hearty converse with God in prayer, is able to pull down what he has been contriving and building many a year."[56] He quotes Ambrose, an early church father, to interpret Paul's prayer—*"The Spirit helps us in our weakness; for we do not know how to pray as we ought, but that very Spirit intercedes with sighs too deep for words"* (Romans 8:26)—"This helping of the Spirit is very emphatic in the original Greek. Like a man taking up a heavy piece of timber by one end, he cannot get it up by himself until some other man takes it up at the other end."[57] This is what the Holy Spirit does with our prayers. And so in the words of the believing heart,

> Faith, mighty faith, the promise sees,
> And looks to God alone;
> Laughs at impossibilities,
> And cries, It shall be done.[58]

So we conclude that God wants "in the gap" prayers, intercessors, prayer warriors, and mediators who will, by their work of faith and labour of love in prayer, hold back judgment, win battles, gain the victory for God and Christ, and break down the walls and barriers that would hinder the gospel. Who wants to sign up?

TWENTY-FOUR

Green-Leaf Christians in a Time of Drought

It is a time of drought. The spiritual watercourses have run dry. The ground is parched and there is nary a green leaf to be found growing anywhere. But there are some sprouts and there is hope. This is how some see it.

The old Liberalism has run out of steam. The evangelicalism of the last thirty years or so is almost spent. There is a new movement in the air. Some call it the emergent church, with new innovations and ideas of spirituality and ways of doing church.

Others are fed up with the cookie-cutter mega-church model, which seems like the model of the few elites among us, realizing that for most churches in North America, Great Britain and Europe, with an average attendance of one hundred or less, it is not going to happen in their community.

There is, however, a desire for an authentic spirituality which seeks to understand Jesus as the gospels show him. This is coupled with a searching and experimentation spirit, which seeks different ways and means of showing the faith to the world of our day than the traditional methods the church has used for the past five hundred years.

Perhaps the Anglican bishop Mark Dyer was right when he said,

> About every five hundred years the Church feels compelled to hold a giant rummage sale... when institutionalized Christianity becomes an intolerable shell that must be shattered in order that renewal and new growth may occur.[59]

This may be such a time.

The rumblings that we are hearing and the sights that we are witnessing are the preparations for the giant rummage sale. The old is being wheeled out on hangers for onlookers to see, sample, and test. The new is being tried, sometimes with an atmosphere of panic, desperation, and crisis. In the words of Bob Dylan's *Like a Rolling Stone*, "When you've got nothing, you've got nothing to lose." Is it true of the western church, according to the story by Hans Christian Anderson, that the emperor who was supposed to have new clothes, really has no clothes but just can't see it yet, or hasn't been told so by an outsider? Has the church been stripped bare and is fooling itself into thinking that all is well? Is the church like Samson, shaking himself after being shorn of his strength saying, *"'I will go out as at other times, and shake myself free.' But he did not know that the Lord had left him"* (Judges 16:20).

But Christians are reading about what's going on. Christians are asking questions about their own church and are freely sampling the changes that other congregations are attempting without worrying about showing their denominational IDs at the door. This is surely a good sign. One church, for example, did a study of *Who Stole My Church*, by Gordon MacDonald.[60]

This was followed up by the more challenging *Life Together* by Dietrich Bonhoeffer.[61] A meeting to consider future leadership needs led to a change of direction and a new focus on youth and families. It's either change or perish.

But there are those who would rather die than change. It is their church, their program, their building, their order of service, and their worship style. If a screen or Power Point should appear, they will be out the door, or at least that's the threat that keeps the leadership from making any moves.

What is to be done? The need is for visionaries who see. The need is for prophets who report. The need is for those with gifts willing to give and to go, despite the atmosphere or conditions holding back spiritual progress. The need is for business people and committed Christians willing to invest financially in the extension of the kingdom of God in the local church and beyond. There must be a willingness to colour outside the lines, or to work outside the normal boundaries and parameters of church life in order to green-up, break forth, and flourish as the people of God.

There may even be the need for some to "bleed" for the church and to give themselves up as the price to pay for the renewal and make-over we so desperately need. Dare we answer God's question to a willing Isaiah, *"Whom shall I send, and who will go for us?"* with *"Here am I; send me!"* and really mean it? (Isaiah 6:8) Only those who like Isaiah have been touched, toughened, and are totally committed would be up to the calling that included the terrible desolation that followed (see Isaiah 6:9-12).

In the meantime, faithful Christians can remain green in the midst of spiritual drought by doing a few simple exercises. Feast on the Word of God and partake in good devotional reading. Find a church where you can be fed. Become a part of a small group fellowship that accepts you as you are. Seek to be true to Christ in all you do. Pray that God will lead you by the Holy Spirit to please him and honour him. Be willing to serve where the Lord has called you and gifted you. Do these things, and the result will be: *"They are like trees planted by streams of water, which yield their fruit in its season, and their leaves do not wither. In all that they do, they prosper"* (Psalm 1:3). The Lord can do this!

TWENTY-FIVE
A New Order

Something is happening to those in the service of Christ. Burnout, depression, breakdown, changing professions, resignation, and withdrawal from volunteer positions in the church are costing a lot. Too few are serving too many, and too many are doing too little about it. We need a new order to be started that is made up of willing workers under a new mandate and with a new motivation for service. It is the mandate and motivation of love.

There is a beautiful Old Testament picture of this in Exodus 21:1-6. A male Hebrew slave is to serve his master for six years, but in the seventh he is to go free without debt. If he has acquired a wife or children by the goodness of his master, they are to remain with the master but he is free to leave. But if he declares that he loves his master, his wife and children, and does not want to go out a free person, *"then his master shall bring him before God [or the judges]. He shall be brought*

*to the door or the doorpost; and his master shall pierce his ear
with an awl; and he shall serve him for life"* (Exodus 21:6). We
could call this the Order of the Pierced Ear.

This is not to suggest piercing or tattooing as a Christian
tradition or habit (for this is prohibited in certain passages,
see Leviticus 19:28), but to understand a new motivation for
serving—love of the Master.

From the New Testament perspective, and in our present situations, many are unsatisfied with their service for
Christ or feel unappreciated for their sacrifice, or are over-
burdened by the workload. Here is a man who after six years
of forced service is treated so well by his master that he
doesn't want to leave him. His response to the offer of freedom is, "I love my master. I don't want to be free, but bound
to him for life!"

The apostle Paul in his letters consistently called himself
a servant or slave (which is the same Greek word) of Jesus
Christ. The slave had no rights, no reason to question his
master and no motivation but to serve obediently unto death.
For the Christian servant, would this not elevate why we
serve and the reason we would want to hang on, whatever the
suffering, difficulties, or sacrifices required? We are not our
own; we are bought with a price. We are protected and shel-
tered by God as we serve him in the cause of the kingdom.
This is a high and holy calling and requires sacrifice and suffering and obedience even unto death, if need be. The service
must certainly be elevated above a willingness merely to help
people or to earn a living for ourselves or our families.

In the Order of the Pierced Ear, it is not the outward appearance of a slave for life that is required, but the inner crucifixion of the self that would want to be set free in order to serve another master—Christ. Paul said three things to the Galatians about his identification with Christ in this way: *"I have been crucified with Christ"* (Galatians 2:19), it is by the cross of the Lord Jesus Christ that *"the world has been crucified to me, and I to the world"* (Galatians 6:14), and *"I carry the marks of Jesus branded on my body"* (6:17).

I think the latter refers to the scars of his many persecutions and sufferings for Christ (2 Corinthians 11:21-33), and not the stigmata or the actual wounds of Christ.

The true servant of the Lord would already have counted the cost of following Christ and the consequences of this on his life, as Jesus clearly taught in each of the gospels (see Matthew 10:32-39, Mark 8:34-38, Luke 14:25-33, and John 12:20-26).

Perhaps the dropout rate or casualties of the spiritual conflict would be lower if Christians first understood that when they sign up spiritually with Jesus, there is no looking back, no longing back, and no going back. It is straight ahead for God and glory, whatever the cost.

> Looking to Jesus the pioneer and perfecter of our faith, who for the sake of the joy that was set before him endured the cross, disregarding its shame, and has taken his seat at the right hand of the throne of God. (Hebrews 12:2)

And the motivation is love. We love our master, the terms of our calling, the work, the benefits, the promises, the fruit, and the hope of our calling. And if there is suffering, persecution, loss, or even death along the way, we have waived our rights to retire, exit, resign, or turn back. We gladly submit and surrender because that is what being a part of the Order requires.

TWENTY-SIX
Unction for Action

Unless there is unction in the pulpit, there will be no action in the pew. As E.M. Bounds has stated:

> What the Church needs today is not more machinery or better, not new organizations or more and novel methods, but men whom the Holy Ghost can use—men of prayer, men mighty in prayer. The Holy Ghost does not flow through methods, but through men. He does not come on machinery, but on men. He does not anoint plans, but men—men of prayer.[62]

The need and the call is for servants of God in ministry or those who are preparing to enter into ministry and preaching to be anointed by the Holy Spirit of God. Only God can give this special touch or unction. No one can describe it, but it is the intangible ingredient that makes preaching and witnessing powerful and irresistible. No force can stand against it or argue it down because no one or nothing can stand against God.

It is given by God only to those who petition and wait for him to pour out his power from on high. The one who has it knows when it is working and effective. Those who hear it consistently can soon detect its absence. The audience senses that God is speaking through his anointed vessel and the individual feels that God is focusing and centering on them particularly.

With the anointing or unction, whatever message is preached, there are results. They may not be visible and there may be no spoken or open response, but God is working deep within the heart and spiritual fruit will follow as surely as day follows night.

Charles Spurgeon, as he ascended the stairs of his pulpit, repeated "I believe in the Holy Ghost," over and over. Of this anointing, he said;

> Such is the mystery of spiritual anointing. We know but cannot tell to others what it is… Unction is a thing which you cannot manufacture, and its counterfeits are worse than worthless. Yet it is, in itself, priceless, and beyond measure needful if you would edify believers and bring sinners to Christ.[63]

This unction is beyond personality, earnestness, preparation, or an impeccable exegesis. It is God impregnating his Word with power and authority. It is the servant who for the time of his or her delivery is controlled and filled by the Holy Spirit in such a way that the Word spoken is literally,

> Living and active, sharper than any two-edged sword, piercing until it divides soul from spirit, joints from marrow; it is able to judge the thoughts and intentions of the heart. And before him no creature is hidden, but all are naked and laid bare to the eyes of the one to whom we must render an account. (Hebrews 4:12-13)

For those hungry for this special gift from God, the advice is simple—wait on God, pray for this anointing, seek Christ and desire him with all of your heart, love God and be willing in all things to give Him the glory, honor and praise, and the unction will come.

As E.M. Bounds again instructs,

> This unction is not an inalienable gift. It is a conditional gift, and its presence is perpetuated and increased by the same process by which it was first secured; by unceasing prayer to God, by impassioned desires after God, by estimating it, by seeking it with tireless ardour, by deeming all else loss or failure without it.[64]

We could say it is the Old Testament unction, or anointing on the prophets, some of the kings, and specially gifted people by the Spirit for holy work. In New Testament terms, we could describe it as the fullness of the Holy Spirit, as was the experience of John the Baptist, Jesus, the Apostles, and Paul. We could also say it is the Holy Spirit who fell at Pentecost who still gifts and empowers his servants and his church to do great exploits for God. But what we are saying is that without unction there is no action and that is what we need—unction for action.

TWENTY-SEVEN
Ultimate Suffering

The Christian will be subject to a variety of suffering throughout his or her earthly sojourn. One form will be a natural or human suffering for being a part of the fallen human race. The apostle Paul told the Roman Christians that the whole of creation is groaning and suffering in labor pains waiting for the Christian's final redemption of the body at the return of Christ (Romans 8:18-25). So the Christian is subject to all of the physical, mental, emotional, environmental, social, economic, political, and religious problems and sufferings that every other human being faces.

There is also a sacrificial and sanctified suffering for being a follower of the Lord Jesus Christ. This will be in the form of rejection, abuse, being ignored, overlooked, and ridiculed by the unbelieving and ignorant world around us. The more serious the believer is about purity of heart and holiness of life, the more the contemporary society and culture will turn away. The writer to the Hebrews said this might happen at the beginning of the Christian life.

> But recall those earlier days when, after you had been enlightened, you endured a hard struggle with sufferings, sometimes being publicly exposed to abuse and persecutions, and sometimes being partners with those so treated. (Hebrews 10:32-33)

The apostle Paul could add his personal sufferings for serving Christ in the church as an example: *"In my flesh I am completing what is lacking in Christ's afflictions for the sake of his body, that is, the church"* (Colossians 1:24). This could include his long list of sufferings in the cause of the gospel (see 2 Corinthians 11:22-29).

There is a soul suffering that is a part of the consecrated believer's life for being separated from the Lord he or she loves. Larry Crabb called it "soul pain"—an emptiness and loneliness, a thirst for God, an inward groaning or a hole that will remain until death.[65] Many Christians do not seem to feel this and want to fill up any moment of stillness or aloneness with activity, noise, or other people or things. Increasingly, many are sensing that what the average church offers, and what Christian devotional literature markets, is not soul satisfying. They are looking for alternative ways of seeking God in other church movements or other spiritual expressions and

traditions, such as what is found in Christian mysticism. As
F.W. Faber writes in his poem, "The Way of Perfection":

> Tis not enough to save our souls,
> To shun the eternal fires;
> The thought of God will rouse the heart
> To more sublime desires.
> God only is the creature's home,
> Though rough and straight the road;
> Yet nothing less can satisfy
> The love that longs for God.
> The perfect way is hard to flesh;
> It is not hard to love;
> If thou wert sick for want of God,
> How swiftly wouldst thou move![66]

And in "Desire for God":

> For the heart only dwells, truly dwells wit
>   its treasure,
> And the langor of love captive hearts can
>   unfetter;
> And they who love God cannot love Him
>   by measure,
> For their love is but hunger to love Him still
>   better.
> God loves to be longed for, He loves to be
>   sought,
> For he sought us Himself with such longing
>   and love:
> He died for desire of us, marvellous
>   thought!

And He yearns for us now to be with Him
above.[67]

The desire for God can reach the point of pain and suffering of soul as expressed by Madame Guyon, in "The Benefits of Suffering":

> By suffering only can we know
> The nature of the life we live;
> The temper of our souls they show,
> How true, how pure, the love we give.
> To leave my love in doubt would be
> No less disgrace than misery!
> I welcome, then, with heart sincere,
> The cross my Saviour bids me take;
> No load, no trial, is severe,
> That's borne or suffered for His sake:
> And thus my sorrow shall proclaim
> A love that's worthy of the name.[68]

There can be a further suffering by the seekers and lovers
of God by means of rejection by those who do not understand the fervour or depth of the devoted heart. But the quest
must go on, even though the road becomes long and lonely.
This can be a deep wound that must be endured while at the
same time loving those who seem to have no interest or desire to follow hard after God. It is the kind of sorrow and suffering experienced by Jesus in the Garden in the words of the
hymn:

'Tis midnight and on Olive's brow The star
    is dimmed that lately shone;
'Tis midnight, in the garden now The
    suff'ring Saviour prays alone.
'Tis midnight, and from all removed Em-
    manuel wrestles lone with fears;
E'en the disciple whom he love Heeds not
    his Master's grief and tears.[69]

The ultimate suffering is that of our Lord Jesus Christ in his passion and on the cross. Not only did it elicit his great cry for release in the Garden of Gethsemane and the sweat-like drops of blood which followed, but the subsequent loud scream in the darkness from the cross. It represented the brief abandonment of his loving Father at the point of becoming the complete and full offering for the sin of the world, when Jesus cried, *"My God, my God, why have you forsaken me?"* (Matthew 27:46).

As his followers, we are not asked to experience the same ultimate suffering in dying a vicarious death for another. This has been done once, for all and forever. Nor are we to share the physical wounds of Christ. However, we must be willing to symbolically take up our cross of obedience and whatever suffering might follow because of that identification. And the ultimate response to that identification is privilege.

TWENTY-EIGHT

Blessedness and Brokenness

Great souls have often been broken before they were blessed. This is a truth authenticated by both Old and New Testament examples. It is easy to point out Jacob as a broken soul as he wrestled with the angel and was wounded in the thigh before he was blessed (see Genesis 32: 24-32). And was Joseph not broken by his descent into the pit, and prison, before his dreams were fulfilled in being raised to the highest place of leadership in Egypt?

Cannot the same be said of Moses, driven into the wilderness for forty years before his call to lead God's people out of Egypt to the Promised Land? What more can be said of others like Abraham, Gideon, Samson, David, Elijah, Isaiah, Jeremiah, and Daniel? And godly women like Sarah, Rebekah, Rachel, Ruth, and Esther all suffered some privation, loss, denial, and brokenness in their seeking God's best for their lives, their families, or their nation and people.

New Testament examples abound of obscurity, suffering, being overlooked, tested, tempted, imprisoned, and killed as a part of being broken before being blessed.

Consider Mary the mother of Jesus, John the Baptist, Jesus, Peter, Stephen, Paul, and John on the island of Patmos. We could even say that brokenness is a blessedness, if it releases us from the slavery to self and opens the door to a wider and deeper ministry of the Holy Spirit.

Sometimes resistance to evil unto the shedding of blood is required for the church of Jesus Christ to be blessed and to move forward. This was true for Stephen the deacon (Acts 6:8 to 7:60) and James the brother of John (Acts 12:2). And holy discipline in the death of Ananias and Sapphira also brought great fear on the whole church and all who heard of it. Great signs and wonders followed and many believers were added to the church (Acts 5:1-16). The blessedness followed the brokenness. This brokenness made people better and bolder as well as being blessed within themselves.

Think of the words of the following hymn of Watchman Nee as an example of the process of God.

> Olives that have known no pressure, no oil
>   can bestow.
> If the grapes escape the winepress, cheering
>   wine can never flow.
> Spikenard only trough the crushing, fra-
>   grance can diffuse.

Shall I then, Lord, shrink from suff'ring
    which thy love for me would choose?
Chorus
Each blow I suffer is true gain to me.
In the place of what thou takest,
Thou dost give Thyself to me.[70]

G.D. Watson captures this kind of special brokenness that leads to blessedness in his tract *Others May, You Cannot*.

If God has called you to be really like Jesus, He will draw you to a life of crucifixion and humility, and put upon you such demands of obedience, that you will not be able to follow other people, or measure yourself by other Christians, and in many ways He will seem to let other good people do things which He will not let you do...

The Lord may let others be honoured and put forward, and keep you hidden in obscurity, because He wants you to produce some choice, fragrant fruit for His coming glory, which can only be produced in the shade. He may let others be great, but keep you small. He may let others do a work for Him and get the credit for it, but He will make you work and toil on without knowing how much you are doing; and then to make your work more precious, He may let others get the credit for the work which you have done, and thus make your reward ten times greater when Jesus comes... He may not explain to you a thousand things which puzzle your reason in His dealings with you. But if you absolutely sell yourself to be His... slave, He will wrap you up in a jealous love, and bestow upon you many blessings which come only to those who are in the inner circle.[71]

TWENTY-NINE
The Healthy Christian

Is good health a blessing or benefit of the Christian life? The apostle John, in his third letter, wrote to his friend and brother Christian Gaius, *"Beloved, I pray that all may go well with you and that you may be in good health, just as it is well with your soul"* (3 John 2). There seems to be something to this. I never knew where it came from, and for many years of ministry I had no clue that it was happening, but I came to realize that there was a truth in the old proverb, "Early to bed and early to rise makes a man healthy, wealthy and wise."

Personally, for many years I have not been a good sleeper, and the early to bed or early to get out of it had nothing to do with health or wealth or wisdom in ministry. But, translated spiritually, it meant that a servant of God in the will of God brings health, wealth, and wisdom to those he or she serves in the congregation or the Christian community.

This is how it was experienced and I forgot to tell the deacons at my church that it would happen there! But I believe it happens everywhere.

HEALTH

Those who faithfully serve the Lord Jesus Christ in their calling will have healthier congregations or followers. It is not that no one will get sick or die, but it will slow down. There will be fewer funerals in the course of the years. As you teach and preach and minister in the name of Christ and in the power of the Holy Spirit, there will be an imperceptible growing and healing process going on. I don't believe it has anything to do with being charismatic or gifted with miracles and healing.

I just began to notice that Christians obedient to the Lord, regular in their attendance, and faithful in their service were healthier, had less sickness, and lived longer. The fitness industry, mental health gurus, and pop psychologists will tell us that this is a normal state of a balanced life. I believe that for Christians and for the body of believers it is the result of Christian health. As pastor Bill Hybels said of his own health, "I've radically altered my eating and exercise habits because exceptional leaders have asked me to consider becoming a healthier person."[72]

I never preached health or healing as such, but I have begun to anoint and pray over the sick who seek the Lord according to James 5:13-18 and with the cooperation of the deacons and elders. It is their ministry, not mine! This is done in a regular worship service and is open to all who wish to come.

"Wealth" is a word which has been abused by the economic times, failing financial institutions, and unscrupulous promoters of their own agendas and kingdoms. But I believe that the Lord's people who are obedient to him can expect a measure of wealth in their lives. Again, this is not to preach a health and wealth gospel, but rather an observation that in the church, Christians are better off and are better able to help others in need because they are the people of God.

In the Old Testament, wealth in the form of possessions, land, divine leading, and victory over the enemy followed being in the will of God. When the people or nation fell from this grace, so did their fortunes. This was evident in the two exiles suffered by Israel and Judah and the terrible things that followed from them. When there was reformation, restoration, renewal, and revival from within and without, wealth in every form followed. The history of the kings and the calling of the prophets to bring them back to God is evidence of this.

And Jesus promised more to anyone who forsook anything for him in this life and much more in the life to come? (See Matthew 13:12, 19: 27-30, 25:29, Luke 6:38.) The giving of God seems to be a result of generosity and benevolence by those so blessed. It is not something earned, asked for, deserved, or expected. Nor is this the so called "faith seed" concept of planting something (monetarily), usually at the urging of a televangelist or fundraiser, and God giving an abundant increase to honour faith. It is just God's blessing and generosity to obedient children in Christ.

WISDOM

Wisdom, as God gives it, seems to be attached to an understanding of his will. To be wise means a believer will grow and mature in knowledge and discernment. It is like the growth of the child and young man Jesus: *"The child grew and became strong, filled with wisdom; and the favor of God was upon him"* (Luke 2:40). *"And Jesus increased in wisdom and in years, and in divine and human favor"* (Luke 2:52).

James tells us that God is willing to give us wisdom generously and ungrudgingly when we ask in faith (James 1:5-8). The writer to the Hebrews said that *"solid food is for the mature, for those whose faculties have been trained by practice to distinguish good from evil"* (Hebrews 5:14). And Paul tells us that if we present our bodies to God, are not conformed to this world, and are transformed by the renewing of our minds, we will be able to discern the will of God—*"what is good and acceptable and perfect"* (Romans 12:2). My experience is that if God's will is not good, acceptable, or perfect for us, it is either not God's will or we are refusing to accept it. Jesus had no problem with this.

This practical wisdom is imparted by God to his inquiring and seeking children. So a Christian whom God is blessing with wisdom will grow spiritually, will mature in Christ, should make fewer mistakes, make better judgments, decide which direction to take, fall into less traps, and be better able to recover when down.

It is a positive attitude of life that makes the Christian walk attractive and gives off an aroma or fragrance of calm, contentment, centeredness in Christ. In fact, Paul said, *"[When] Christ leads us in triumphal procession, and through us spreads in every place the fragrance that comes from knowing him… we are the aroma of Christ to God among those who are being saved and among those who are perishing… Who is sufficient for these things?"* (2 Corinthians 2:14-16) Amazing!

So those in Christ should be healthier, wealthier, and wiser. This is how to be a healthy Christian. God just gives it!

THIRTY
Only Jesus

There are many today who ask, "Why do I have to believe only in Jesus and use his name all the time? Can't I just believe in God like everybody else and get to heaven? Aren't we all the same and going to the same place?" The answer is the same as it was in Jesus' time and has to do with Jesus' own words in the gospels and in the other epistles.

Every Christian is to believe about Jesus what the following Scriptures affirm:

Only Jesus became God in the flesh for all (Colossians 2:9, John 1:14).

Only Jesus came into the world to die for sin (1 Timothy 1:15, 2:5-6).

Only Jesus gave his life and died for us on a cross, was raised the third day, and was seen alive by many witnesses (1 Corinthians 15:1-8).

Only Jesus said, *"Believe in God, believe also in me"* (John 14:1).

Only Jesus said, *"I am the way, and the truth, and the life. No one comes to the Father except through me"* (John 14:6). See also the other exclusive claims of Jesus' "I am's" in John's gospel: *"I am the bread of life"* (6:35, 48), *"I am the light of the world"* (8:12, 9:5), *"Before Abraham was, I am"* (8:58), *"I am the good shepherd"* (10:11, 14), *"I am the gate for the sheep"* (10:7), *"The Father and I are one"* (10:30), *"I am the resurrection and the life"* (11:25), and *"I am the vine"* (15:5). In John's Revelation, it is written, *"I am the Alpha and the Omega"* (1:8).

Only Jesus promised to come back to earth and take us to be with him (John 14: 2-4, Acts 1:11, 1 Thessalonians 4: 13-18, Revelation 1: 5-8).

Only Jesus is the *"name under heaven given among mortals by which we must be saved… there is salvation in on one else"* (Acts 4:12).

Only Jesus said he had all authority and power in heaven and earth, and commissioned his followers to go into all the world and make disciples of all nations, baptizing them in the name of the Father and of the Son and of the Holy Spirit, and teaching them to obey everything he commanded and said he would be with them to the end of the age (Matthew 28: 18-20).

These and many other texts give us the unalterable truth that belief and trust in the Lord Jesus is the only way to know God, to please him, to obtain salvation, and to go to be with him in the end. The apostle John summarized this truth so well in his gospel.

> He [Jesus] was in the world, and the world came into being through him; yet the world did not know him. He came to what was his own, and his own people did not accept him. But to all who received him, who believed in his name, he gave power to become children of God, who were born, not of blood or of the will of the flesh or of the will of man, but of God. (John 1:10-13)

Therefore, the focus of the whole Christian life is unashamedly only Jesus. He is to be believed on, received, loved, obeyed, served, and lived for in this life. The Christian is then to wait for His return in power and great glory when God will subdue all things under Jesus and give him a kingdom with all who believe, of which there will be no end. This is the Christian's hope.

But there is also a warning that goes along with the invitation and the hope.

Only Jesus can give eternal life to whomever he pleases.

Only Jesus has the power to raise the dead.

Only Jesus has authority from the Father to judge everyone (John 5:19-30).

Only Jesus has been exalted to the highest place and given a name that is above every name.

Only Jesus will have all in heaven and earth and under the earth bow the knee to him.

Only Jesus will have every tongue confess that he is Christ the Lord, to the glory of the Father (Philippians 2:8-11).

This is a very serious exclusivity that is claimed for Jesus and those who believe on him and call themselves Christians.

There needs to be a great humility, graciousness, and love in communicating these truths to others who do not believe the same. And the church and Christians have not always been tolerant or patient or accepting of differences in belief. So when Jesus says, by way of invitation, *"Come to me, all you that are weary and are carrying heavy burdens, and I will give you rest"* (Matthew 11:28), we recognize that not all will come. Some will turn away, some will be angry, some will persecute. But we are still like Jesus, to love, while at the same time believing that the real key to life and eternal life is Only Jesus.

ENDNOTES

[1] Scriptures taken from Romans 9:1-2, 10:1, 8:17; Lamentations 5:16-17; Psalms 74:9-10, 85:6; Habakkuk 3:2; Song of Solomon 1:6, Amos 7:14-15, Habakkuk 2:1; Micah 6:8, Ezekiel 33:30-33; Jeremiah 8:20; Isaiah 57:1; Jeremiah 8:22; Lamentations 3:21-23; Jeremiah 29:11; Lamentations 5:21; Psalms 115:1; Isaiah 35:8, 30:18-19, 56:13; and Matthew 23:37-39.

[2] *The Book of Common Prayer*, The Order for Morning Prayer, p. 7. The Anglican Center, Toronto, nd.

[3] Revised from an article originally printed in *The Atlantic Baptist*, August, 1989, p. 41.

[4] G. Lloyd Rediger, *Clergy Killers: Guidance for Pastors and Congregations Under Attack* (Louisville, KY: Westminster John Knox Press, 1997).

[5] William Barclay, *The Daily Bible, The Gospel of Mark*, rev. ed. (Toronto, ON: G.R. Welch, 1975), p. 140.

[6] Malcolm Muggeridge, *A Third Testament* (New York, NY: Ballantine Books/Random House Inc., 1976), p. 68.

[7] Thomas A. Kempis, *Of The Imitation of Christ*, Trans. by Abbot Justin McCann (New York, NY: New American Library, Mentor-Omega Books, 1957), p. 37.

[8] Chris Tomlin, *The Way I Was Made* (Sisters, OR: Multnomah Publishers, 2005), p. 78.

[9] "And Can It Be That I Should Gain," by Charles Wesley, The Hymnal, The Baptist Federation of Canada, 1973, Carol M. Giesbrecht, Editor, No. 90.

[10] Fred Buechner, *Listening to Your Life, Daily Meditations*, Compiled and Edited George Connor (San Francisco, CA: HarperCollins, 1992), p. 205.

[11] "All of Self and None of Thee," by Thomas Monod, The Hymnary for Use in Baptist Churches, Toronto: Ryerson Press, 1936, No. 323.

[12] John Milton, *Paradise Lost and Paradise Regained,* Ed. Christopher Ricks (New York, NY: Signet Classic, New American Library, 1968), Introduction, p. xxv.

[13] Source—Wikipedia, "Samuel Johnson."

[14] William Barclay, *The Daily Study Bible, The Letter to the Galatians and Ephesians*, rev. ed., (Burlington: G.R. Welch, 1976), p. 156.

[15] Ibid.

[16] *Tyndale New Testament Commentaries, Ephesians*, Intro. and Commentary Francis Foulkes, (Grand Rapids, MI: Wm. B. Eerdmans Pub., Co., 1975), p. 133.

[17] John R.W. Stott, *God's New Society, The Message of Ephesians, The Bible Speaks Today* (Downers Grove, IL: Inter-Varsity Press, 1979), p. 186.

[18] Source—Wikipedia, "Edmund Burke."

[19] *The Atlantic Baptist*, nd.

[20] Dietrich Bonhoeffer, *Life Together*, Trans. with Introduction John W. Doberstein (New York, NY: Harper & Row Pub., 1954), Introduction, p. 8.

[21] http://www.acts17-11.com/cross.html

[22] David Watson, *Discipleship* (London: Hodder & Stougton, 1981), 75-77.

[23] Henry Scougal, *The Life of God in the Soul of Man*, Pamphlet (London: Inter Varsity Fellowship, 1962), pp. 11-12.

[24] http://www.bible.ca/b-new-testament-documents-f-f-bruce-ch6.htm

[25] Timothy Dudley Smith, *John Stott, The Making of a Leader, A Biography, The Early Years* (Downers Grove, IL: Inter Varsity Press, 1999), p. 457.

[26] Thomas Reeves, *The Empty Church, The Suicide of Liberal Christianity* (New York, NY: The Free Press, 1996).

[27] Ibid., p. 209.

[28] George Jones, Choices, http://www.metrolyrics.com/choices-lyrics-george-jones.html

[29] Sheldon VanAuken, Under The Mercy (Nashville, TN: Thomas Nelson Publisher, 1985), pp. 94-101.

[30] "Art Thou Weary? Art Thou Languid?" Verse 5. Based on the Greek of Stephen the Sabaite (725-815). Hymns of the Christian Life (Harrisburg, PA: Christian Publications, 1962), p. 290. Trans. John M. Neale (1810-1866).

[31] "Just As I Am" (Hymn), Charlotte Elliott, Wikipedia.

[32] "Am I a Soldier of the Cross?" by Isaac Watts, The Worshipping Church, A Hymnal (Carol Stream, IL: Hope Publishing Company, 1990), No. 668.

[33] Source—Wikipedia, "Helen Roseveare." Sermon Index.net audio sermons, "The Cost of Discipleship."

[34] Source—Wikipedia, "Joni Eareckson Tada."

[35] Source—Wikipedia, "William Whiting Borden."

[36] "On Living by God's Guidance." Printed sermon by the Rev. John N. Gladstone, Yorkminister Park Baptist Church, Toronto, February 24, 1974. #52, p. 4.

[37] Julia Keay, *Alexander the Corrector* (London: Harper-Collins, 2004), p. 120.

[38] Source—Wikipedia, Inspiring missions slogan and notable quotes from missionaries—Jim Eliot.

[39] Source—Wikipedia, "Robert Browning." AskOxford: 100 Classic Quotes.

[40] Source—Wikipedia, Pierre Trudeau quote.

[41] James Luther Mays, *Psalms, Interpretation, A Bible Commentary for Teaching and Preaching* (Louisville, KY: John Knox Press, 1994), p. 322.

[42] Donald Coggin, *The Sacrament of the Word* (London: Collins, 1987), pp. 21-22.

[43] Lancelot Andrewes, *The Private Devotions of Lancelot Andrewes,* Selected by David A. MacLennan (New York, NY: World Publishing Co., 1969), pp. 35, 38.

[44] http://www2.ljworld.com/news/2000/aug/06/preside ntial_personalities/?more_like_this

[45] M. Scott Peck, The Road Less Travelled and Beyond, Spiritual Growth in an Age of Anxiety (New York, NY: Simon & Schuster, 1977), p. 82.

[46] Ibid., pp. 82-84, paraphrased.

[47] Abbe de Tourville, *Streams of Grace*, ed. and trans. Robin Waterfield (Glasgow: Collins, 1985), p. 43.

[48] *Great Writings of Goethe*, Ed. & Intro. Stephen Spender (New York: The New American Library, 1958), 25.

[49] Emily Dickinson, *Selected Poems* (New York, NY: Tom Doherty Associates, Inc., 1993), p. 8.

[50] Muggeridge, Ibid., p. 68.

[51] Richard Holmes, *Coleridge, Early Visions* (London: Penguine Books, 1989), p. 171.

[52] Michael Stancliffe Sermons, Symbols snd Dances (London: SPCK, 1986), p. 2.

[53] Annie Dillard, *For The Time Being*, (Toronto, ON: Penquin Books, 1999), p. 72.

[54] Pierre Burton, *The Joy of Writing* (Toronto, ON: Doubleday Canada), 2003, p. 105.

[55] R. Arthur Matthews, *Born for Battle* (Colorado: OMF Books, 1978), p. 118.

[56] David M'Intyre, *The Hidden Life of Prayer* (Minneapolis, MN: Bethany House Publishers, 1993), p. 16.

[57] Ibid., p. 44.

[58] Google, Religious Quotes, Charles Wesley.

[59] Phyllis Tickle, *The Great Emergence, How Christianity is Changing and Why* (Grand Rapids, MI: Baker Books, 2008), p. 16.

[60] Gordon MacDonald, *Who Stole My Church?* (Nashville, TN: Thomas Nelson, 2007).

[61] Dietrich Bonhoeffer, *Life Together* (New York, NY: Harper & Row, 1954).

[62] E.M. Bounds, *Power Through Prayer* (London: Marshall Brothers, Ltd. Publishers, nd.), p. 10.

[63] Ibid., p. 87.

[64] Ibid., p. 98.

[65] Larry Crabb, *Real Church: Does It Exist? Can I Find It?* (Nashville, TN: Thomas Nelson, 2009), pp. 107-113.

[66] A.W. Tozer, *The Christian Book of Mystical Verse* (Harrisburg, PA: Christian Publications, Inc., 1963), pp. 51-52.

[67] Ibid., pp. 54-57.

[68] Ibid., p. 81.

[69] "Tis midnight and on Olive's brow," by William Tappan, The Hymnal, Baptist Federation of Canada, 1973, ed. Carol Giesbrecht, No. 79.

[70] "Olives that have known no pressure." Hymns (Los Angeles, CA: The Streams Publisher, 1966), p. 626.

[71] Source—

www.savedbygrace.blogspot.com/2009/04others-may-you-cannot

[72] Bill Hybels, *Axiom: Powerful Leadership Proverbs* (Grand Rapids, MI: Zondervan, 2008), p. 23.